SOCIETY & CHILDREN'S LITERATURE

Society & Children's Literature

PAPERS PRESENTED on research, social history, and children's literature at a symposium sponsored by the School of Library Science, Simmons College, and the Committee on National Planning for Special Collections of the Children's Services Division of the American Library Association, May 14–15, 1976

EDITED BY JAMES H. FRASER

David R. Godine · *Publisher*
in association with the
American Library Association

First published in 1978 by
David R. Godine, Publisher
306 Dartmouth Street, Boston, Massachusetts 02116

Main entry under title:
Society & children's literature.
    Includes bibliographical references and index.
     1. Children's literature, American—Congresses.
  I. Fraser, James Howard, 1934–
 II. Simmons College, Boston. School of Library Science.
III. American Library Association. Committee on National
    Planning for Special Collections of Children's Books.
PN1009.A1S63   028.5   77-94110
ISBN 0-87923-236-6
ISBN 0-8389-3213-4 pbk

PRINTED IN THE UNITED STATES OF AMERICA

CONTENTS

INTRODUCTION *by James H. Fraser*   vii

1. AMERICAN SOCIETY AS REFLECTED IN CHILDREN'S LITERATURE: Some Introductory Comments to the Symposium on Research, Social History, and Children's Literature *by Frances Henne*   1

2. CHILDREN'S LITERATURE AND AMERICAN CULTURE 1820–1860 *by Anne Scott MacLeod*   11

3. SOCIAL FACTORS SHAPING SOME LATE NINETEENTH-CENTURY CHILDREN'S PERIODICAL FICTION *by R. Gordon Kelly*   33

4. REGIONALISM IN AMERICAN CHILDREN'S LITERATURE *by Fred Erisman*   53

5. FOREIGN LANGUAGE PUBLISHING FOR CHILDREN IN THE UNITED STATES: A Comment on Yiddish, Estonian, Ukrainian, and Armenian Materials *by James H. Fraser*   77

6. IN FOR A PENNY, IN FOR A POUND: Or, Some Economic Aspects of Collecting Eighteenth- and Early Nineteenth-Century Books for Children, with Reflections on the Sources of Such Books, the Prices Now Paid for Them, and the Best Remedy for the Pain Those Prices Give the Purchaser, All Simply Stated by a Long-Sufferer *by Howell Heaney*   93

7. RANDOM NOTES ON THE PRESERVATION OF EIGHTEENTH- AND NINETEENTH-CENTURY CHILDREN'S BOOKS *by Frederick E. Bauer, Jr.*   103

8. PECULIAR DIFFICULTY: A TALE OF THE EIGHTEENTH CENTURY: Being an Account of Some Lamentable Lacks, Together with a Few Desperate Needs *by Gerald Gottlieb*   119

9. MANUSCRIPTS OF CHILDREN'S LITERATURE IN THE BEINECKE LIBRARY *by Marjorie G. Wynne*   137

10. LOST INNOCENCE IN THE AMERICAN COMICS *by Walter Savage*   151

11. FILM ARCHIVES: UNEXPLORED TERRITORY *by Marshall Deutelbaum*   167

12. SUMMARY AND COMMENTARY *by Frances Henne*   181

APPENDIX 1: Genesis of a Research Collection *by Philip J. McNiff*   189

APPENDIX 2: Symposium Program   195

CONTRIBUTORS   199

INDEX   201

INTRODUCTION

Interdisciplinary symposia for researchers with a special interest in literature for young people are European phenomena of comparatively recent origin, the Mainau Conferences (Federal Republic of Germany) being the first.[1] Subsequent conferences on the Island of Mainau met annually through 1968. The proceedings were published regularly and dealt with such subjects as youth books and the mass media, the youth book in the east and west, and youth literature and its critics, to name but three. Since 1968, the *Arbeitskreis für Jugendliteratur*, together with the German Section of the International Board on Books for Young People, has continued these annual conferences.

In the period of the 1960s an increasing number of individuals and organizations throughout Western Europe established symposia for the continuing benefit of scholars in various disciplines and for their colleagues engaged in the service of young people, e.g., teachers, librarians, psychologists, booksellers. Among the better known was the Frankfurter Kolloquium,[2] which developed into the biennial symposium of the International Research Society for Children's and Youth Literature. The first of the International Research Society for Children's and Youth Literature symposia was held in Frankfurt in 1971,[3] and they have taken place since then in Boldern, Switzerland, and Södertälje, Sweden.

In 1966, 1967, and 1970 a series of symposia were held in Denmark on the theme of literature for children and young people as a means to promote international understanding; these meetings also brought together a varied group of research specialists and service-oriented participants.[4]

Many are familiar with the annual conferences (usually held in Austria) of the International Institute for Children's and Youth Literature and Reading Research in Vienna. Researchers from Western European countries attend and address themselves to various questions concerned with youth literature, reading interests, and reading problems.

To be sure, symposia on children's and youth literature have been held in the United States since the mid-1950s; yet they have been oriented primarily toward the needs of children's librarians and teachers. Since the early 1970s organizations such as the Modern Language Association, the Popular Culture Association, and the American Psychological Association have been responsive to children's literature interest groups and have scheduled papers on children's literature within their respective programs; but here again, the audience has been restricted to the interest of a specific discipline.

The Simmons College symposium on research, social history, and children's literature—the papers of which are presented here—was in the tradition of the European approach. The Boston gathering brought together researchers from various disciplines outside the field of education as well as librarians and individuals engaged in service to children.

A brief note on the development of the Simmons symposium: Professor Frances Henne (Columbia University) and I discussed for several years the need to initiate in this country symposia such as this. The idea was presented as a possibility to the National Planning Committee for Special Collections of the Children's Services Division and to the Board of Directors of the Children's Services Division of the American Library Association. The support of the Committee and the Board resulted in the formation of a subcommittee for planning. An offer of sponsorship by Drs. Robert Stueart and Timothy Sineath of Simmons College School of Library Science was accepted. After much work on the part of Dr. Sineath and others, the plan became a reality. It is hoped that this symposium will establish a precedent for its type in this country where, all too often, research and service-oriented personnel have little opportunity to talk with one another and to benefit from such exchanges.

Regarding the sequence of papers in this publication, it should be stated that we followed, with modifications, the order in which the papers were presented, the exception being the placement in an appendix of Philip McNiff's extemporaneous talk at the Boston Public Library. Dr. Edgar Mayhew, Professor of Art at Connecticut College in New London, Connecticut, and Jane C. Nylander, Curator of Textiles at Old Sturbridge Village, Massachusetts, each gave an informal slide presentation. Reporting the discourse without benefit of the necessary illustrations would serve little purpose and has therefore been excluded from the proceedings. Dr. Mayhew spoke on American interiors as seen in nineteenth-century children's books and Miss Nylander addressed the issue of the validity of children's book illustration as social documents. Following Marjorie Wynne's presentation, Barbara Bader gave a talk on the nature of her research for her book, *American Picturebooks from Noah's Ark to the Beast Within* (New York: Macmillan, 1976). Miss Bader requested that these informal comments be excluded from the published symposium.

I wish to thank Barbara Festa and Ursula Sommer for editorial assistance.

—James H. Fraser

NOTES

1. The first Mainau Conference was organized in 1954 by the International Centre Castle (Island of Mainau) under the auspices of The World Alliance of the Young Men's Christian Association.

2. Klaus Doderer, ed., *Jugendliteraturforschung International Schwerpunkte und Richtungen Frankfurter Kolloquium,* 1969 (Youth Literature Research International: problems and trends). (Weinheim: Verlag Julius Beltz, 1969).

3. Klaus Doderer, ed., *Internationales Symposium für Kinder- und Jugendliteratur und Lesersoziologie,* 1971 (Contribution on Children's Literature and Reader Sociology). (Frankfurt/Main: Internationale Forschungsgesellschaft für Kinder- und Jugendliteratur, 1972).

4. *Contributions made to the Seminar at Skarrildhus September 1970 on Literature for Children and Young People as a Means of Promotion of International Understanding.* (Copenhagen: Danish UNESCO Schools Project, 1970).

I.

AMERICAN SOCIETY AS REFLECTED IN CHILDREN'S LITERATURE

Some Introductory Comments to the Symposium on Research, Social History, and Children's Literature

FRANCES HENNE

Research relating to social history and children's literature represents an area of inquiry, exploration, and reflection that is distinct from the bibliographic, literary, critical, and chronological works, commentaries, and appreciations which constitute the bulk of our writing about children's literature. With the ever-increasing interest of social historians, sociologists, anthropologists (moving beyond folklore), psychologists, librarians, and specialists in art, English, and other disciplines in exploring the many facets of this broad spectrum, the subject of social history and children's literature currently constitutes a very active field for scholarship and research.

So far, this research has tended to concentrate on society as reflected in children's literature. Only recently have we begun to be concerned, from a variety of angles, with children's literature as reflected in society. The scope of this symposium shows both kinds of reflections upon its mirror. The symposium also recognizes the necessity to interpret children's literature in its broad context, embracing not only books but also other types of print and media formats other than print. Selected for discussion are books, periodicals, illustrations, comic strips, and films. If time permitted, many other types of children's literature could receive our attention: television and radio programs, recordings, games, computerized materials, ephemera (including the books, cards, or other formats that are packaged with commercial products or issued separately as advertisements—a field sadly neglected by scholars), and many others. Oral narration and locally produced materials, including books written by children (now receiving considerable commercial emphasis and promotion) form other examples. The emphasis of this symposium falls upon American society and publications, but resources from countries other than the United States and the foreign language press and children's literature in this country are included. The time range is a broad one.

The diversity of the research becomes quickly apparent in the classifications that can be made overviewing the field. (One such classification could be constructed of the varied types of methodology used in research studies, several of them represented in the papers presented at this symposium.) For the purposes of my introductory comments, I would like to underline this diversity by noting, briefly and unscientifically, some areas of actual and potential research dealing with American society reflected in children's literature and some areas of activity dealing with children's literature reflected in American society. The categories in these classifications of topics are not discrete, and they cover all time periods and all media formats.

Aspects of American society reflected in children's literature include the following examples (the list is not definitive): The education of youth in school is revealed in a variety of resources. Teaching techniques can be ascertained from the vehicles used for teaching reading, arithmetic, science, and other skills and subjects. Analyses of textbooks provide information about the content of the curriculum and can be equally illuminating in determining what is omitted. (A tendency to concentrate on what is included in literature for children, with little or no attention paid to what is omitted—which in many cases may be even more significant—is characteristic of a great deal of research in the field.) Analyses of assignments, of materials used by students in completing assignments, of materials other than textbooks recommended by teachers in lists, bibliographies, or in other ways, and of multimedia 'packages,' whether commercially or locally produced, to be used in connection with independent and individualized learning give further insights into curriculum content. Although not children's literature, instructional resources for teachers—units of instruction, curriculum guides, lesson plans, teaching aids and devices, and many other types—form important sources of information about both teaching techniques and curriculum content. These resources are too often neglected in our research and also in the collections of research libraries.

General knowledge forms an arbitrary category to cover instructional children's literature that is not directly school related. (Educational, instructional, and didactic are all amorphous terms that can be and have been applied to all children's literature.) These materials, which embrace both nonfiction and fiction, give some idea about what society considers important for children to know and what society thinks might interest children. In fiction, the information is obviously presented in such typical examples as the travel fiction books of the nineteenth century, those 'walks' and 'talks' with some knowledgeable adult where children's questions about nature, or science, or whatever are answered fully and promptly in books of bygone centuries, and career novels of relatively recent vintage; it is deviously presented in many teen-age novels and so-called realistic fiction for children today.

Manners and deportment, whether in treatises focusing directly on the subject, in cautionary tales, or in incidental mention in other works, reflect the social etiquette of a given period.

Moralistic, ethical, and behavioral values (the consideration of mankind) in children's literature give evidence of many aspects of society and the changes that have occurred over the years: existing social problems; dangers and temptations confronting youth; developmental values for youth; prevailing attitudes toward other countries and toward minority or ethnic groups (inquiries dealing with stereotyping, chauvinism, nationalism, and internationalism form a rich vein in research studies); the attitudes of children toward parents, teachers, the law (the vigilante motif runs rampant in children's literature), and other adults and social institutions; and the significance attached to and the treatment of such wide-ranging topics as the work ethic, money, success, poverty, wealth (the rich child in children's literature merits further study), family life, violence, cruelty, kindness, moral codes, social justice, and so on. Here, too, would be those studies dealing with personal heroes and heroines (one wonders whether the heroes and heroines in popular series books are judged by their young readers to be characters to be admired and emulated or just to be well-liked people). As time has passed, would our research show that we have witnessed the transfiguration of hero and heroine into merely protagonists?

Patriotism and nationalism are reflected in different ways, one of which has already been noted. One of the earliest purposes in the teaching of reading in this country was aimed toward instilling and strengthening the patriotic spirit. Symbol and other analyses that describe the nature and extent of the portrayal of these concepts in children's literature form one avenue of research; another deals with the number, kind, and source of works for children translated into the national language of a country (the global view would be illuminating), and also with how these works are translated—a currently active arena of inquiry and heated discussion; and a third relates to the topic to be discussed by Mr. Fraser during this symposium—the foreign language press and children's literature in the United States, which holds implications for similar studies in other countries.

History is portrayed in one way or another in all categories, and is isolated for mention here primarily to emphasize the desirability of knowing what aspects, events, or persons of history are covered or not covered, what biases are observable, and what historical methods are employed. The treatment of war, national heroes, socio-economic conditions, international relations, forms of government, and many other topics can reveal significant characteristics of the social history of different countries and different periods of time. The effects of revisionism can be detected in children's literature, and this topic is now in its second cycle of research.

Pastimes and recreation, hobbies, and sports are shown in nonfiction works dealing with these subjects, in other nonfiction, and in fiction. The subjects, themes, and values are legion in number. Always of interest, possibly only to academicians, are those inquiries that report any mention in children's literature of reading and books.

The arts and humanistic values in children's literature receive attention in some of the Symposium papers, as does the art of the picture book. This category and that of science have such broad parameters that time permits no more than this mere mention of them.

Portrayal of daily life in children's books presumably reflects the contemporary scene: the family setting, activities of children, the treatment of children, living conditions, dress, and other elements. Parts of this overall category form the focus of two of the Symposium papers; other segments are mentioned in other papers. Does sex come within this category, elsewhere, or constitute a separate one? Unquestionably, in children's literature, both nonfictional and fictional, it has its own social history.

Other categories include contemporary events, with particular reference to the content of periodicals, newspapers, and newscasts designed for children (again, what is omitted and what viewpoints are presented?); religion and religious themes (other than Sunday School literature, which has been a popular subject for study, little serious research has been undertaken in this area); and humor (a provocative and practically untilled area for research). Although animals are not totally excluded from the categories that have been noted, the vast and popular domain of animal stories and characters in children's literature merits much fuller treatment.

Popular culture is grouped separately here because the literature represented therein forms a distinct category in many ways, not the least of which are popular appeal, widespread accessibility, and often popular prices. No matter what the time period, we have tended to have some form of mass media. Here would fall such diverse items as the series books, comic strips and comic books, the big-little books, animated (or mechanical or movable) and 'gimmick' books, certain games and toys, items that children collect, TV tie-ins, personalized books, most Disney items, hit records, popular songs, McLoughlin books, Golden Books, dime novels, popular TV and radio programs, popular movies, and the like. (Do we now include CB radio?) These communications have reached the largest audiences of children. In libraries for children, in histories and commentaries dealing with children's literature, and in collections of research libraries, these materials have been excluded or accorded too little attention, and yet the contents of these materials, with their huge audiences, surely hold significance in the research, analysis, and interpretation of children's literature. 'Bad Books for Children' form an important area for research.

The list of categories in the above classification of topics is neither discrete nor definitive. This observation applies also to the second part of my introductory comments, children's literature as reflected in American society.

The importance attached by adults to children's books and other media can be ascertained by studies of the quality and quantity of libraries for children, of bookstores, and of other outlets. (One cannot help but be gloomy about our society's attitude toward children's books and reading when one becomes aware of the widespread lack of support of libraries for children in this country.)

The importance attached by children to the various media formats has relevance: their reading, viewing, and listening patterns, interests, attitudes, preferences, and interpretations.

Publishing and production of children's literature form part of the picture—content and quantity of materials, sales and distribution, structure and policies, and many other factors.

In another context, mention has already been made of the reflection of adult attitudes toward children in children's literature, as shown in the status of children, their role in society, and other ways. Not unrelated would be the undue perpetuation of childhood, as it were, through writing down (the young adult novel, for example) and similar treatment in films and other media. Exploitation of children can be detected in commercialism that takes advantage of a popular market and publishes/produces what sells, regardless of worth or quality; in advertising, whether advertising series titles in the text of every title of a series, television and periodical advertising directed toward children, or other kinds; and also in the ways that some adults artificially use or condemn children's books in connection with their social viewpoints or platforms.

Children's literature has been reflected in the dress of children (à la Buster Brown, Little Lord Fauntleroy, Kate Greenaway, to name a few); in language, sometimes literally (the special languages that occur in some fantasies), sometimes metaphorically (references to Pollyanna and others), and many times as part of a working vocabulary, with examples that can be drawn from many children's classics, comics, and television and radio programs; in popular art/artifacts, including pictures, statues, china, watches, and innumerable other objects—the creations of Disney, Schulz, and Potter seem to be replicated everywhere. This list could be extended to include songs, toys and games, customs, and food.

Censorship, the evaluation and selection of children's literature, and children's literature as a scholarly discipline form important and significant segments of our subject. The last-named involves not only research and opportunities for study of children's literature but also the bibliographic apparatus and resources necessary for their pursuit, topics which are included in the program of this symposium. In conclusion, let it be stated that the occurrence of this symposium considerably enhances the status of children's literature as a scholarly discipline.

2.

CHILDREN'S LITERATURE AND AMERICAN CULTURE

1820-1860

ANNE SCOTT MACLEOD

The United States in 1820 was a nation still new to nationhood and already caught in a swift tide of change. When Washington Irving, writing in that year, referred to the 'great torrent of migration and improvement, which is making such incessant change in . . . this restless country,' his description was surely no more than accurate.[1] For with the Peace of 1815, which closed the second British-American war, the country entered upon an era of great economic and physical expansion. The forty years from 1820 to 1860 were a boom time (though punctuated by periodic financial collapses), during which the American population grew by more than 200 percent, national territory increased enormously, and technology transformed the character of the economy. The evolution of an agrarian nation into an industrial and urban society was underway and proceeding at a remarkable pace. In fact, the salient observation to be made about many of the changes of the era has less to do with their nature than with the rate at which they took place. The pace was headlong throughout the antebellum period.

Strain and unrest accompanied change; socially, economically, and politically, Jacksonian society was turbulent. In addition to the growth that affected so many aspects of the new nation, the period was marked by the excitements of evangelical religion, by an astonishing wave of reform movements, and most of all, by the ever more acrimonious debate over slavery, the issue which by 1860 overwhelmed all others and brought the young republic to civil war.

American reaction to the ferment of the time was mixed. On the surface, optimism and a buoyant sense of national pride prevailed. Americans believed energetically in their country; they were proud of its recent past and convinced of the promise of the future. The rhetoric of the period generally celebrated the progress, the prosperity, the democratic spirit, and the opportunity offered by American society.

At the same time, Jacksonian Americans felt the anxieties that inevitably afflict those who live in times of rapid change. Pride in

13

the past and hope for the future were alike tempered by apprehension lest the promise of America be somehow betrayed. Even while they moved with their society, responding vigorously to economic and social opportunity, many Americans also yearned toward the stability of the past, and worried over the direction of the future.

When an American fictional literature for children began to be written, about 1820, it was distinctly a product of its time. It reflected the intense interest in family and childhood that was to mark all of the nineteenth century, and it reflected too the sharpened nationalism so characteristic of the Jacksonian era: imported children's stories, like other foreign influences, Americans now thought inadequate to the needs of a republic. 'Foreign books . . . are not to be proscribed,' one author conceded, 'but it is absurd that they should be made, among our children, the main standard of feeling and thought.'[2] By the second quarter of the century, national feeling required that books for American children should be home products.

But it was undoubtedly the American preoccupation with the future that was the strongest impetus behind the development of a non-school juvenile literature before 1860. The children who were to inherit the republic were increasingly the object of adult attention on that account. As the fiction created for them reveals, they were the repository for much of the optimism of the Jacksonian period and for many of its anxieties as well. Written out of a concern for children and country, the literature could not but embody something of its authors' expectations and apprehensions for the future of both. And so it did: in the hundreds of storybooks published in the United States between 1820 and 1860 is a record of what adults wanted of and for the next generation. Less directly, but just as surely, the books offer insight into what Americans wanted of and for their society.

The connections between this literature and its background are not always immediately obvious, however. To examine in detail the juvenile fiction of antebellum America is to enter a twilight world, a world that seems at first almost wholly sheltered from the robust life around it. The tensions and turmoil of Jacksonian society seem remote, the arguments muted. Although they were produced in a nation experiencing great and rapid change, the children's stories were static and repetitive. There were few departures from conventional opinion, few surprising points of view. Controversy was as rare as genius in the literature.

The focus of the stories was extremely narrow. They were written to teach, and specifically, to teach morality. All Americans of the period agreed that a high level of individual morality was indispensable if the promise of the nation's future was to be fulfilled. The nature of American institutions was settled, they believed; what remained was to make them work, to insure that the republic survived. 'It is not now to be made a question whether our political institutions are right or wrong,' wrote one early author of children's fiction. 'Education is to be conducted with reference to honor and usefulness under these institutions as they are, and to the sentiments on which they depend for permanent support.'[3]

It was clear to thoughtful Americans that the permanent support of democratic institutions lay in public virtue and equally clear that public virtue depended upon the character of private citizens. Thus the developing moral character of children was the object of much anxious attention in the period. Education, whether home or school, was primarily *moral* education—in part, of course, for its own sake, but also because only the firm establishment of exemplary character in the rising generation could secure the future of the republic.

Children's fiction before 1860 was written entirely as an adjunct to such moral education. Every other consideration was secondary, if indeed other considerations figured at all. The authors wished to be entertaining, but only just enough to attract child readers, that they might be instructed in morality. They were wary of the 'gaudy' allures of 'high-wrought wonder,' and of the improbabilities of old folk tales. William Cardell spoke for them all when he scornfully discarded 'Blue Beard . . . [and] fiddling cats . . . [and] motherly talking goats' in favor of 'fidelity to nature, to moral truth; regard to the public good [and] the endearing scenes of domestic life.'[4]

All the writers were as earnest. These sober stories, each leading to a moral lesson, were written to provide children with models of virtuous living. Moral didacticism was their sole reason for being, as the authors often told their young readers directly: 'When I tell you stories of things that never happened,' Samuel Goodrich explained, 'my real design is to give you lessons of importance.'[5] It would not have occurred to the authors to doubt that fiction could shape character; they believed deeply in their mission. 'If one pair of erring feet may be turned into the path of obedience and peace by means of my story,' said the author of *Self-Willed Susie*, 'the end for which it was written will be accomplished.'[6]

No doubt because their purposes were so selective, authors gave scant attention to the settings of their narratives. It would be difficult to construct from the literature a picture of the physical surrounding of the stories, to come away from them with a feeling for the communities, the houses, the schools that made up a child's landscape in the period. There were few homely details of food or dress or common activity to anchor the fiction to a particular time and place; most stories were played out against backgrounds almost abstract in their generality. Unlike the richly detailed, often autobiographical children's fiction of later years, early juvenile tales said little about the daily business of growing up in an American household during the first half of the nineteenth century. The evocation of a way of life that can be found in such books as *Tom Sawyer*, *Little Women*, Aldrich's *Story of a Bad Boy*, or Eggleston's *Hoosier Schoolmaster*, simply does not exist in juvenile literature before 1860.

Characterization and plots were purposefully flat. Nineteenth-century theorists of child nurture were tireless in pointing out that children learned much better by example than by precept, and early nineteenth-century authors were equally tireless in their efforts to provide the examples which would edify the young. Since complexity could only have obscured the messages, characterization was simple and it was always easy to identify the good and bad models. Lazy, fretful Louisa was contrasted with her cheerful, industrious cousin, and the story showed how the differences in their temperaments shaped their lives.[7] An honest, temperate youth was seen to thrive, while the deceitful lad who stole his father's rum and so succumbed to drink, went from bad to worse and ended wretchedly, in prison.[8] In story after story, good character was contrasted with bad, and appropriate conclusions drawn.

It should be said that the fiction was usually optimistic about the possibility of reforming the bad examples. Though some errant characters proceeded briskly from early mistakes to an untimely end, many more were salvaged, quite often by the good examples, who frequently talked in moral precepts at the same time they demonstrated sound character. One outstanding boy reformed an unpromising acquaintance in a matter of a few weeks, by talking 'much and very sensibly' to him.[9] Good children sometimes even led adults to a better way of life in the fiction, though of course in such cases they worked by 'the silent power of example alone,' since it would hardly have been fitting for a child to lecture an adult, no matter how helpfully.[10]

Narratives were staid, domestic, and predictable. Each tale centered on a child in need of some moral correction; the correction of this or that fault then constituted the whole plot. Since most authors theoretically favored the idea that experience is the best teacher, what small excitement there was in the stories was furnished by the consequences of childish misbehavior. A girl whose fondness for sweets took her into the pantry by night to lick the honey jar managed to burn down the house with the candle she left there. A boy who skated on thin ice against all parental warning fell through and narrowly escaped death by drowning. There was, in fact, a plethora of narrow escapes in the literature, all fitting and frightening results of moral error. But near-disaster was usually close enough. Though wrong-doing always had consequences, preferably vivid and more or less logical, the punishment was not often extreme—just inevitable. The authors, of course, were not really willing to let experience speak for itself, however loudly. They underlined the moral conclusions for their readers, suggesting that while the fictional children learned from painful experience, readers could be forewarned and spared much misery by listening to their elders in the first place.

All juvenile fiction before 1860 was much the same: simple narratives, always pointing to a moral, featureless backgrounds, stock characters moving through patterned plots. It is startling to contemplate how much was left out, for all the authors' claims that they wrote about reality.

Except for frequent and pious references to George Washington, the American past was largely ignored. The pioneer struggle against the wilderness, which was to provide material for hundreds of children's books in later times, was never the subject of these early tales. In fact, wilderness was hardly mentioned at all; it would have been impossible to discover from children's stories the enormous expansion to the West that took place in the period. The American Revolution, in its rare appearances, was not an occasion for adventure tales, but for close and earnest reasoning about the moral implications of war in general.

In the same way, slavery was all but invisible in juvenile fiction, though it was the issue that dominated American political debate from 1820, the year of the Missouri Compromise, to 1860, the eve of the Civil War. Even when it was inserted into stories by authors who were dedicated abolitionists, the mention was usually mild and indirect—small clue to the bitter struggle that was to split the nation.

Industrialization and urbanization, both important trends in the period, were equally elusive in the fiction. Most writers of juvenile literature regarded cities with suspicion, if not with outright hostility. They saw them as dangerous, corrupting and immoral, and rarely made them the background for their narratives. As cities grew, so did the authors' mistrust. By the last decade of the period, though cities were the locale of more stories, they were almost always portrayed as terrible testing grounds for the home-learned morality of fictional heroes and heroines. The best advice in most juvenile books suggested that all Americans were better off in the country, which was both moral and healthy, than in cities.

As for factories, though their role in the economy expanded steadily after 1820, they were given no place at all in most children's books before 1850. Even in the fifties, there were only a few direct references to industry; most writers continued to idealize the yeoman farmer as the backbone of the nation at a time when it was already becoming apparent that the nation's economic future lay in another direction.

Yet in spite of these and other silences, the juvenile literature of Jacksonian America does speak both of and for its time. In special and frequently oblique ways, it furnishes clues to the feeling life of the society that produced it. Though its recording of factual reality was sketchy and certainly selective, as a chronicle of emotional reaction, it is eloquent. What the fiction speaks of is not so much what happened in the period as what many quite representative middle-class Americans *felt* about what was happening. It tells of their pride in the United States and in its institutions and its recent past, and it says much about their hopes for the future. But pride was accompanied by uneasiness as social change hurtled on, and hope was shaded by anxiety—and the juvenile stories carried doubtful messages as well. When American writers undertook the moral and social instruction of children through fiction, they necessarily documented their own attitudes, both conscious and unconscious, toward childhood and society. If we look at these, and at the historical context in which they were expressed, we can begin to read, in and between the lines of children's fiction, a story more interesting and more moving, in its own way, than any the authors consciously wrote.

Attitudes toward childhood, for example, determined both the form and the tone of juvenile literature. Moral didacticism reflected accurately the prevailing ideas of adults about both the nature of children and the purposes of childhood. The fiction was usually optimistic about child nature. Again and again, the stories tell of children who were 'for the most part good,' but who were 'possessed of one great fault' (or two or three): a mix, in other words, of good and bad; imperfect, but not beyond hope of redemption. Though the old Calvinist concept of infant depravity lingered on in some quarters and was expressed occasionally in some of the children's books published by denominational presses, in general a more benign view dominated by 1830. Without much theoretical struggle, most Americans had by that time adopted the opinion that children came to the world with potential for both good and evil, and that the direction of their lives depended heavily upon the training they received in their years of growing up. Thus the note of optimism that undergirded the steady moralizing of the books. If the nature of children was not evil inborn, but neutral or potential, then character could surely be influenced for the good by wise and conscientious adults. Children could be made Christian, as Horace Bushnell suggested, without the conversion experience, through home training alone.[11] Thus, too, the sense of urgency that made of every childish experience an opportunity for teaching morality. That urgency, and the characteristically sober tone of all the literature, were natural consequences of the authors' view of the purpose of childhood, which was serious in the extreme. Childhood was wholly preparation, entirely a moral training ground for adult life. Frivolity, imaginative play, and uninstructive entertainment were dismissed, not so much because they were sinful as because they wasted the brief, precious time in which a child must learn so much that was so important. The idea of childhood as a period of intrinsic value, full of joy and free of care, was not yet.

The ideals of moral character set out in the children's fiction are also revealing at several levels. The virtues recommended to young readers were many and various, but they fit into a general pattern. All were in the direction of order, restraint, stability, and a strong sense of social responsibility as the age interpreted it. Obedience was the most fundamental virtue for a child to acquire: few stories closed without at least one salute to its importance. Clearly, obedience was paramount because it provided the necessary framework within which all other morality could be taught. Even more important, order within the family, which obedience implied, was a paradigm for order in society: 'The obedience of children to their parents is the basis of all government,' observed one author,[12] and most writers of juvenile fiction agreed. The inheritors of the American Revolution were anxious indeed to secure social order in their own time.

Besides obedience, always the signal virtue, self-control, usefulness, charity, and a willingness to put the wishes of others above one's own were the character traits most consistently recommended in the literature. All of these emphasized regard for other people, and the books affirmed that commitment in explicit and highly exaggerated terms. To live 'for others,' children were often told, was the only sure way to contentment. As one fictional mother told her daughter, 'You can never be unhappy while you do everything that is in your power for others, without the hope of recompense.'[13]

Logically enough, the faults the literature scored most relentlessly were opposites of the virtues it praised. Selfishness was the greatest and most encompassing failing; to look to one's own advantage was always suspect in children's stories. Ambition or any form of competitive spirit was equated with selfishness and equally condemned. Contentment, rather than striving, was idealized. Juvenile fiction frequently advised children to be satisfied with what they had, instead of chasing after the uncertain rewards of fame and fortune. Many stories warned that 'restless seeking' could yield no permanent prizes; boys in particular were cautioned against the dangers of leaving home to pursue wealth and advancement. Ambition, symbolized by soldiering and seafaring and city employment, was dangerous; safety and moral certainty were better guides to happiness, according to the fiction.

In short, the idealizations in children's fiction ran directly counter to the prevailing direction of change in Jacksonian society. The moral values set out in the literature were a kind of mirror image of the most apparent realities of the period — and therein, of course, is their connection with that turbulent time. The exuberance of the young United States, its social fluidity, its fiercely competitive spirit, and its mounting tensions rarely appeared directly in juvenile fiction, yet they were all there in the reverse images of order, cooperation, and sober attention to duty and conscience that were repeated in every book. Clearly, the authors were reacting against the alarming tendencies of their society by idealizing virtues that would counterbalance the dangers as they saw them.

Faced with disorder and instability, they valued predictability and order; living with ceaseless change, they idealized certainty. As physical migration separated families and splintered communities, the fiction urged children to stay close to home. As economic life shifted toward cities and factories, stories warned of the spiritual hazards of the city, and extolled the independence and morality of a farmer's life.

Most insistent of all was the drive in the fiction to counter the growing materialism and the rampant competitiveness of American society. Here was the source of the constant admonitions to children to live 'for others'; here the reason for the ubiquitous anxious warnings against 'selfishness' and the repeated assurances that only care for others could bring happiness. The material ambition that all observers, foreign and American, saw as the hallmark of the Jacksonian age was steadily repudiated in children's fiction: fame was ephemeral, success might be reversed overnight, wealth could never insure contentment. Not the rich but the good were happy, children's stories said, not personal attainment but cooperation and responsibility toward others were worthy goals in human life.

The effort to impart these attitudes to children was always marked with some anxiety. The authors had few illusions that the world beyond resembled their idealized home: as one fictional mother observed, 'The principles which wisdom and truth sanction are not those which govern society.'[14] If a child was to acquire firm moral principles, he must do so early, in the brief years before he left home.

The aim was independent moral strength. Though the writers constantly pointed out that obedience to parents was the 'first law in life' to children, a careful reading of the fiction makes it clear that the real goal of child nurture was not so much to make children amenable to adult authority as to create in them a reliable inner direction as early as possible. It was not at all uncommon for stories about children as young as four or five to record long, grave conversations between parent and child in which the child's moral behavior was meticulously weighed and judged.[15] Such home training was to provide a child with a moral gyroscope, an unshakable center from which his behavior would always proceed, that he might 'pass unscathed through the temptations of the world.'[16] And though that moral strength might begin in parental direction, it would not remain dependent upon it, nor, indeed, upon any outer authority.

For outer authority was precisely what American life could not be counted upon to provide. The freedom of Jacksonian society, however often they praised it, also alarmed many Americans, certainly including many of those who wrote for children. The absence of a fixed social order, the lightness of the law, the fluidity of economic and social life, all threatened to leave individuals without defined relations to one another or to the larger world in which they all must live. Opportunity and ambition unrestrained threatened to reduce American society to a desperate struggle for advantage.

The counter the children's fiction posed to this awesome freedom was an idealized self-control, an inner discipline each person imposed upon himself which would meet the challenge of a changing social order. If the outer world could not be frozen into predictable form, the inner world of moral character might be, provided the effort was made early and earnestly enough. The whole point of childhood training as children's authors saw it—and therefore the whole point of children's fiction as they wrote it—was to develop in children that sensitive conscience, that internalized set of principles that would make them morally self-sufficient. Then, and only then, could American society live with its freedom without descending into social anarchy.

Yet to point out connections between an anxious, unsettled society and a didactic, moralizing literature for children is not to suggest that the literature was nothing more than an effort at 'social control.' It was that, of course, but it had other qualities as well.

No one can make a claim for the literary merit of this fiction: there was none. But there was a certain dignity and conviction in it that went beyond a simple attempt to control society by indoctrinating children with safe moral values. The attitude the fiction displayed toward its child audience was kindly, on the whole, and in some ways more respectful than it has been in many children's books since. However much they may have overestimated children's interest in ethical questions, the authors took them seriously as moral beings. If we find their attention to matters of childish right and wrong overly solemn and heavy-handed, still we can recognize that it was an attitude more willing to acknowledge a child's human dignity than, say, the sentimental vision that dwelt upon children's charm and innocence, or the condescending view of them as 'cute' and amusing to adults.

And surely the virtues the fiction hoped to instill in children were more than trivial. Moral self-reliance, inner independence, kindness, responsibility, and a decent regard for the needs of others—these qualities transcend the limited aims of adult convenience and societal 'law and order.' Even for us, a century and a half older as a nation and far removed from the simplistic moral outlook of early nineteenth-century juvenile fiction, it may be possible to agree with the authors who thought such virtues sound qualities for the citizens of a republic.

↑ ↑ ↑ ↑ ↑

PARTICIPANT: *If the settings in these children's books are so bland and featureless, how do you differentiate between the American literature and the English literature of the same period?*

MACLEOD: It is a subtle question and difficult to answer. It was one I worried about greatly when I started out, but curiously enough, the internal evidence is really there. Sometimes it is very obvious. When you find a child chastised for lying on her bed 'waiting until the servant came and dressed her,' you aren't dealing with an American story, in all probability. There were occasional local references, though they were rarely specific. Sometimes the name of a town was given, or references to 'how fortunate we all are to live in New England.' Generally, the books of this period give no feeling for the details of living in a given place at a given time, and little sense of the pattern of a child's daily life. It is strange how little the community was reflected in most of this literature. I noted Dr. Kelly made similar observations in his book talk. The church as an institution is not usually mentioned. The literature is suffused with a generalized religious moral tone, but only rarely does anyone actually go to church or see a minister in a story. Even mention of school is infrequent. However, schools did provide a good clue to locale if mentioned. An American school was distinctly different from a British school of the period.

PARTICIPANT: *Dr. MacLeod, you said to live for others was a frequent theme and emphasized this. Was this true for both male and female children, or was it essentially one or the other?*

MACLEOD: It was true for both. I saw very little open differentiation between boys and girls on this question. I think there is a subtle and assumed difference about the audience of the books which is reflected partly in the number of characters in the books who were girls. Sometimes there are references to girls learning certain household duties that were not expected of boys, though boys were sometimes told that it was, on the whole, good for them to know how such things were done. In fact, I found them interestingly non-sexist sometimes; for example, in the matter of explanations of the technical matters. Even today if a child in a book asks a question requiring a technical answer, he will often be sent to his father. Not so in the books of the period under discussion. The mothers were full of long disquisitions on the heavens and the movement of the planets or the names of minerals. The aunts were remarkable sources of information. We do have a number of false assumptions about the literature of the period.

PARTICIPANT: *Did you find mention of what the children themselves were reading aside from the references to Maria Edgeworth?*

MACLEOD: Of course I was alert to this, having worked with children's literature for many years. There were very few. I was surprised how often Maria Edgeworth's name did come up in the few times that reading was mentioned. I don't ever recall anyone saying that he or she had read any books of folk tales. Such mention was like everything else in the books. If there, it was there for a purpose. If a child were to mention it at all, he would say something to the effect of how happy he was to have one of Miss Edgeworth's lovely little books. There wasn't much of that, however.

PARTICIPANT: *Are you saying then that fables were probably not read much at that time? I thought that maybe they might have been more exaggerated. You also alluded to this quality of selfish-*

ness. Recently I was in a discussion of 'The Little Red Hen' where the teacher was discussing the 'good' version versus a 'bad' version. The quality of selfishness in these little animals was accentuated in one version and a more Americanized version of a later edition only alluded to it. I am wondering if this was more of an eighteenth-century or early nineteenth-century carry-over?

MACLEOD: Regarding fables: I'm sure that children read fables, but there was very little mention of it. You have to remember that most of the authors who were writing these books were uneasy with the idea of a child having access to that kind of literature. In fact, one of the reasons they were writing the dismal little tales was to save children from the 'corrupting influence' of the older stories. And put in context, that is not as odd as it sounds. Most of what was available was not as thoroughly edited or modified as we see it in children's anthologies today. The traditional folk material available then was in fairly blunt form. I did find some books of fables rewritten, but I wasn't primarily interested in that area; I was concerned mainly with original fiction; however, those few tales I found generally had been altered. I feel that folk literature, like any literature, varies in quality. I think that most of what we see in forms for children has been skillfully rearranged; editing for literary purposes must be done. You would hardly offer it to anyone in its pure form, as taken down on a tape recorder. In the first place, it's rambling; often it appears to have little point. Usually if it is part of a living body of folklore, it has innumerable subplots; and much of it is quite candid in its references to sexuality.

PARTICIPANT: *Who were the chief printers, publishers, distributors of children's books at that time?*

MACLEOD: I don't think I can recite a list of them from memory. I would refer you to the bibliography in my book. Some names come quickly to mind—Lee and Shepard, Carleton and Porter, and of course the American Sunday School Union, which published vast quantities and was by far the largest.

PARTICIPANT: *You mentioned that most of the fiction is basically realistic, modified realism in any case, and that there was some rewriting of fables. Was there anything written during that period that you would classify as 'American' fantasy?*

MACLEOD: Yes. If you stretch the edges of the category out, there were a few. There was one story by a man named Cone, something called 'The Fairies in America.' It was a didactic tale. It was cast into a vaguely fairy-story form; that is, there was a moralizing fairy who accompanied the child character wherever he went. Once in a while a mild allegory would be published. But there was very little because it was not approved. Fantasy was viewed as dangerous. Parents worried about children staying in contact with reality. They didn't feel it would do any good to encourage them in flights of fancy. And they didn't.

PARTICIPANT: *You mentioned earlier that most of these stories lacked a strongly American background. Didn't these authors see themselves as writing American literature for American children?*

MACLEOD: The answer has to do with ideals, and I probably should have said that one of the strong bits of internal evidence has to do with the egalitarianism that comes into many of the books. Sometimes it is very self-conscious—you feel it is being put on like a shirt. But the idea is that snobbism, the notion of class and rank, is not really fitting for an American child, and the issue of rank was a complicated question. Authors were willing to say that rank existed, but the reader was not to assume too much on that account. Rank wasn't to exist in school except on merit. One's sense of where one belonged shouldn't give one a feeling of superiority. On the contrary, if one were conscious of being a different (higher) rank from someone else, that underscored responsibility rather than superiority. As I think about it, there is another bit of internal evidence. The uncertainty of any economic position was a constant theme in many of the books. One might be comfortable today, but not necessarily tomorrow. There was a realistic view. One of the reasons constantly mentioned for learning the useful arts was that one never knew what next week would bring. If one were living in a fine house today, one might have to do one's own washing tomorrow. Reasons for the writing of American literature were highly theoretical. The purpose was not to acquaint an American child with his country in a physical sense, but with its morals, with American principles—as Cardell said somewhere.

PARTICIPANT: *I think you mentioned one of the purposes of the author's function was to create an atmosphere which would prevent future anarchy. Is there something in British literature that reflects an effort to repair the loss of the Colonies?*

MACLEOD: The question is whether there is any distinction between American and British literature on the purposes of an inner direction. I think that is how I understand your question. I'm inclined to say I don't know the British literature well enough to answer definitively. I've read it—some of it. There certainly are interesting distinctions, but how they relate to the loss of the British colonies, I couldn't conceivably make a guess without much, much firmer grounding in the literature.

PARTICIPANT: *In general the people in England are not particularly aware that the loss of the land in America was so important. And the average person as reflected in the children's book would not have been aware of the fact that they lost anything particularly good. Did they? Even Mrs. Ewing, who was so identified with the British nation and Empire and who wrote so much about it, never even mentions the conflict in America.*

MACLEOD: That ties in with the fact that contemporary with the loss of what became the States was the gaining of Australia and India, which was much more glamorous. So there was a movement toward the East, which was exactly occurring with the loss of the New England colonies. A very interesting question, but one on which we could only speculate until we had read a fair amount of the literature. I don't feel that I am in any position to comment on it.

PARTICIPANT: *I'm interested in having the children's literature of this period placed in the context of the adult popular fiction of the time. Could you comment on the relationship?*

MACLEOD: Yes. This was the beginning of the era of the domestic novel, you remember, and in that sense the children's books and the adult books do share some ground—the preoccupation with family and home; the books that many women wrote for a female audience. In fact, many times the authors who wrote for children also wrote adult popular novels. There were also some didactic novels for adults that were strikingly similar to the children's literature in some way. Stylistically, however, it is not easy to characterize the popular literature of the period as a unit. Much of the popular literature was becoming melodramatic and sensational. That is not true, however, of the children's literature until the 1850s. For most of the period, the romanticism and the sensationalism of the adult popular literature did not find its way into the children's literature.

PARTICIPANT: *You treat the forty years as a homogenous period with only moderate change. I wonder what you see as the major differences in the literature of the early 1820s in comparison with the later 1800s?*

MACLEOD: Actually, in my book, I did make a distinction between what happens in the fifties and what happened in the rest of the period, although there is little carry-over. The type of literature being written in the twenties, thirties, and forties, goes right on being written in the fifties. But in addition to that a different kind of literature develops that is much closer to the more sensational type of literature that we see after the Civil War. There are hints of Alger themes. There are also children's novels that are similar to the melodramatic domestic novel in which a 'soap opera' type of woman appears. In the earlier literature, the position of 'Mother' was very strong, but it was restrained, rational, and Edgeworthian, if you will. But a transition is taking place by the fifties. A much stronger social consciousness begins to develop, although not a very positive social consciousness.

Much of it comes from economic changes. You have a reflection of desperation about the old ideas of individual charity being the real solution to poverty. That doesn't fit anymore in the fifties.

PARTICIPANT: *I was wondering if you could comment on the appearance of social Darwinism in children's literature—when it was considered acceptable to be competitive.*

MACLEOD: Obviously, if it is social Darwinism, it comes after the period I am talking about, if ever it does with wholehearted approval. On competition, I think what you find is an uneasy coexistence of the notion of consideration of other people, and the striving for individual success. In these books to some extent, and I think slowly over the period, the balance shifted between which was the more important. I don't think that many children's books applaud the concept of social Darwinism without reservation in any period.

NOTES

1. Washington Irving, *The Legend of Sleepy Hollow*, quoted by Leo Marx in *The Machine in the Garden* (New York: Oxford University Press, 1964), p. 3.

2. William Cardell, *The Happy Family*, 2d ed. (Philadelphia: T. T. Ash, 1828), p. 4.

3. Ibid.

4. William Cardell, *Story of Jack Halyard*, 3d ed. (Philadelphia: Uriah Hunt, 1825), p. ix.

5. Samuel Goodrich, *Parley's Book of Fables* (Hartford: White, Dwier and Co., 1836), p. 6.

6. *Self-Willed Susie and Her Sister Lena* (New York: Carleton and Porter, and American Sunday School Union, 1860), p. 150.

7. Lydia Maria Child, ed., *The Juvenile Miscellany* (Boston: John Putnam, 1826–1834, 3d ser., 2 [1832]), p. 225.

8. Joseph Alden, *The State Prisoner* (New York: Love and Tippett, 1848).

9. William Cardell, *Story of Jack Halyard*, p. 26.

10. See Aunt Friendly, *Bound Out* (New York: Anson D. F. Randolph, 1859).

11. Horace Bushnell, *Christian Nurture* (New Haven: Yale University Press, 1947).

12. *Filial Duty Recommended and Enforced* (New York: O. Scott, 1847), p. 4.

13. Clara Arnold, ed., *A Juvenile Keepsake* (Boston: Phillips, Sampson and Co., 1851), p. 57.

14. Catherine Maria Sedgwick, *Conquest and Self-Conquest* (New York: Harper and Bros., 1843), p. 55.

15. See, for example, *Little Mary, A Story for Children from Four to Five Years Old* (By 'A Mother') (Boston: Cottons and Barnard, 1831).

16. *Alfred Raymond* (Philadelphia: American Sunday School Union, 1854), p. 5.

3.
SOCIAL FACTORS SHAPING SOME LATE NINETEENTH-CENTURY CHILDREN'S PERIODICAL FICTION

R. GORDON KELLY

In a recent review of *Mother Was a Lady* (my study of American periodical fiction for children after the Civil War), Bernard Wishy makes a sharp and invidious distinction between my analysis of the fiction and the theoretical and methodological issues that I discuss.[1] He seems to approve of the former but dismisses the latter as 'intrusive' and frequently at odds with the analysis of the fiction. He implies that the theoretical assumptions, drawn 'hither and yon' from several disciplines, lack coherence. More is at issue than coherence, however. Professor Wishy implies that possessing a 'sensitive imagination' counts for more than having, and specifying, some clear-cut assumptions—a position that seems to me utterly wrongheaded.

In its original form, and as initially revised following the acceptance by Greenwood, the manuscript for *Mother Was a Lady* contained a longish theoretical introduction in which I set forth the assumptions about culture, society, and literature that had shaped my analysis of the children's periodical fiction in very direct and decisive ways. For reasons that were never satisfactorily clarified, Greenwood refused to accept this theoretical introduction, except in a highly generalized and attenuated form. Just before the book was published, a condensed version of the original introduction appeared in *American Quarterly* under the title 'Literature and the Historian.'[2]

Had Professor Wishy's review not happened along so fortuitously, I should probably have had to invent him for this occasion; I cannot 'summarize the purpose and theme' of *Mother Was a Lady*, as Jim Fraser has asked me to do, without establishing a context for the study—and without some discussion of theory. The study was shaped by several influences: by Stow Persons' formulations concerning the existence of a nineteenth-century gentry elite, which he subsequently published in 1973 as *The Decline of American Gentility*;[3] by John Cawelti, whose notion of popular narrative formula constitutes the conceptual basis for his recent study of popular literature *Adventure, Mystery and Romance*;[4] and by Alexander Kern, who introduced me to the sociology of knowledge and speculated about its relevance for literary history. More broadly, the study was shaped by the need in American Studies to formulate more precisely and satisfactorily the relationship between literature, culture, and society than had characterized earlier work in the field. Such a reformulation was, in part, a problem in theory—or less grandly and perhaps more accurately—a matter of clarifying and articulating assumptions. Contrary to what Professor Wishy implies in his review, theory and analysis are inseparable. One does not, cannot, undertake analysis without theory—though a great deal of analysis proceeds from implicit theory and unexamined assumptions. By looking at children's literature, I hoped to test some ideas about the relationship between literature, culture, and society as well as to describe salient characteristics of a particular body of narrative fiction—narrative fiction because stories tend to link behavior and consequences quite directly; the stories we tell ourselves seem to me a richly allusive—if elusive—source with which to explore definitions of appropriate and inappropriate behavior. As for choosing fiction for children, the most succinct justification has been stated by James Spradley, a cultural anthropologist: 'The richest settings for discovering the rules of a society are those where novices of one sort or another are being instructed in appropriate behavior.'[5] Literature for children is one such setting, if it can be established that a primary intention of its creators is to instruct; but because we have no way to measure or reconstruct the influence of literature on children in the past, except in an anecdotal fashion, I concentrated on exploring the relationships between fiction for children and the adults who created it. Finally, the choice of the several periodicals used in the study—*Youth's Companion*, *St. Nicholas*, *Wide Awake*, the *Riverside Magazine for Young People*, and *Our Young Folks*—was dictated by my conviction that valid generalizations from literary evidence depend on specifying the social group with which an author identifies. If there was an American gentry elite, as Professor Persons argued, and if they produced literature for children, then their values, attitudes, and beliefs would presumably be especially clear in that literature. *St. Nicholas* and the other periodicals selected for study appeared to issue from such a group, a cultural elite centered geographically in the largest cities of the eastern seaboard, whose ideal of social identity was an Americanized version of the Christian gentleman and his lady. A major aspect of the study was to determine to what extent, and in what ways, the concept of gentility shaped the fiction in the several periodicals during the generation following the Civil War. In effect, Professor Persons's concept of a gentry elite functioned as a low-level theory that defined a range of questions which I brought to the fiction: Are ladies and gentlemen depicted in the fiction? If so, how? What are their functions? and so forth.

But, in addition to drawing on the concept of a gentry elite, I was guided in my research by arguments put forth by Peter Berger and Thomas Luckmann in their essay *The Social Construction of Reality.*[6] Time permits only the most general statements about a subtle, complex, and controversial argument. The authors contend that the worlds in which men have their being are socially constructed in certain crucial respects. By this they mean that essential elements of our environment are structured systems of shared meanings, that these systems are maintained by consensus, and that they are specific to groups of people located in place and time. These 'worlds,' or 'symbolic universes,' to use their phrase, are created, maintained or altered, and transmitted by means of symbol systems. The most important of the symbol systems implicated in creating and maintaining social reality is, of course, language. It follows that these socially constructed 'worlds' are arbitrary and precarious because their specifics—of belief and behavior—owe little, if anything, to man's instinctual nature. Behavior, Berger and Luckmann insist, is structured by cultural, rather than biological, imperatives.

At this point we may seem to be a long way from literature. We can move a step nearer the pages of *St. Nicholas* and the other children's periodicals by considering the implications of these highly generalized assertions for the process of socialization. In man, the biological basis of what we call *culture* permits enormous variation in customary behavior. Socialization, the process by which one becomes a functioning member of a group, is productive both of individual identity as well as of the continued existence of the group. The process of 'primary' social-ization—the child's basic induction into the group ways—is likely to be a source of tension and concern in any society. A considerable measure of success in the socializing process—a marked conformity to behavioral norms as well as the *desire* to conform with a minimum of compulsion—is a necessary condition for maintaining the existence of a group at the level of behavior but more especially at the level of value and belief. Socialization becomes especially problematical, and a source of severe tension, when alternative values and beliefs are available for emulation—as they are in complex modern societies. The agents of socialization are then under greater pressure to transmit intact the meanings which structure their world. Although the principal agency of primary socialization in our society has been the family, the mass media (including books and periodicals for children) are clearly implicated, in several ways, in the overall socialization process.

'Critical and imaginative works,' the critic Kenneth Burke tells us, 'are answers to questions posed by the situation in which they arose. They are not merely answers, they are *strategic* answers, *stylized* answers.'[7] In a generic sense, the 'situation' to which Burke refers may be understood to be the precarious, socially constructed reality described by Berger and Luckmann. The specific 'situation' which posed questions for an American gentry elite in the nineteenth century was a fluid, competitive, rapidly expanding egalitarian society in which gentry definitions of appropriate behavior and appropriate values were challenged by alternative modes of behavior and alternative symbols. More-over, insofar as America was in Lincoln's phrase 'the last, best hope of mankind'—and insofar as its children *were* its future—a great deal appeared to be riding on the successful socialization of Young America. The fiction addressed to children by the gentry constitutes a series of complex symbolic acts by which they (1) affirmed the values and beliefs which gave meaning, purpose, order, and identity to their lives; (2) competed commer-cially and ideologically with other forms of literature available to children; and (3) identified those whose alternative values threatened gentry influence and identity. In brief, the fiction for children produced under gentry auspices must be seen essentially and fundamentally as a series of efforts over time to transmit their culture to another generation. Their stories, which they told themselves and to their children, are acts of a certain kind, designed to effect certain ends, and shaped by certain influences. It is not a 'sensitive imagination' but theory which defines them so.

Now, it should be clear that these ideas have methodological implications. They also have implications for developing research collections, a point to which I shall return after summarizing some of the main points of my analysis of narrative fiction in *St. Nicholas* and the other periodicals in the period 1865 to 1890.

In these periodicals, there are two sorts of stories—two highly conventionalized narrative formulas or patterns. One I call the Ordeal. In this type of story, a child or young person becomes isolated temporarily from the protection and influence of adults, generally parents. Circumstances require the child to act decisively. Often the child has very little time in which to act appropriately; the situations appear contrived to emphasize that sound character rather than sound reasoning are involved. The child proves herself in action and returns to the safety of the family and a suitable reward.

'Nellie in the Light-house,' a *St. Nicholas* story published in 1877, exemplifies the Ordeal formula.[8] Nellie is the seven-year-old daughter of a lighthouse keeper, a widower who employs an elderly black couple to care for the household. Soon after the story opens, Nellie's father goes to the mainland for supplies and the housekeeper is called away to nurse a neighbor. A squall blows up, the housekeeper's husband collapses with a stroke, and Nellie must somehow find a way to rekindle the beacon, extinguished when a window broke. Mastering the panic which threatens to overwhelm her—and to which her brother succumbs—she recalls a hymn her mother used to sing to her. Her anxiety subsides; she recalls that pine knots will burn, even in a wind; and she successfully rekindles the light. Her prompt action saves her father, who had been caught in the squall as he was rowing back to the lighthouse. Courage, self-reliance, and presence of mind are qualities most often emphasized in the Ordeal.

The second formula characteristic of the gentry children's periodicals following the Civil War I call the Change of Heart. Like the Ordeal, the Change of Heart story generally involves separation, isolation, and eventual incorporation. Unlike the Ordeal, however, the Change of Heart involves a child who has not yet achieved the self-discipline and sound moral character which constituted the gentry ideal. A key element in the Change of Heart stories is a conversion experience—a significant shift in perception—in the course of which the erring child realizes that her behavior is unacceptable, and usually harmful, and she consciously resolves to change her ways. Authors usually took care to show the better behavior—the outward sign—that expressed and validated the inner change. Representative of the Change-of-Heart formula is 'Charlie Balch's Metamorphosis,' which appeared in Horace Scudder's *Riverside Magazine for Young People* in 1867.[9] Charlie is a sullen, lazy, withdrawn boy whose mother is dead. His father, a politician with little time to devote to this son, has sent him off to boarding school, where Charlie quickly falls in with a rough crowd. The boy's change of heart occurs during a sermon when he suddenly recognizes that 'probably there is no such thing as an indifferent moment— a moment in which our characters are not being secretly shaped by the bias of the will, either for good or evil.'[10] Radical improvement in character is possible in these stories, but it is a gradual process, and in this instance Charlie's resolution must be tested. By the end of his metamorphosis, Charlie displays better manners, a more cheerful disposition, even a more comely appearance. His successful redemption, the author suggests, provides a lesson in the responsibility for aiding others which those of 'gentle feeling' must accept.

The traditional virtues ascribed to the gentleman—fortitude, temperance, prudence, justice, liberality, and courtesy—are given differential emphasis in the body of fiction selected for study. Daniel Sharp Ford, the editor of *Youth's Companion* from 1857 until his death in 1899, insisted on stories which involved lively, rapid action—the kind of tale in which courage might well play a conspicuous and appropriate part but in which an emphasis on courtesy and manners would be less likely. Moreover, courage, self-reliance, and presence of mind are the qualities demanded by the social realities depicted in the stories. It is a precarious world, filled with hidden dangers and deceptive appearances; and in their fiction, the gentry continually counseled courage and prudent forethought. Change-of-Heart stories, however, do not reveal a symmetrical distribution of proscribed traits when compared with stories of the Ordeal type. Cowardice is rarely shown changing to fortitude. Rather the focus is on self-centeredness and a child's lack of self-discipline. Stories frequently dramatized the unfortunate consequences of careless, reckless, and irresponsible behavior as well as the inevitable suffering brought on by pride and other forms of ungentlemanly and unladylike self-assertiveness. So great was the emphasis on self-control that one author warned that 'carelessness is worse than stealing';[11] and Louisa May Alcott assured the youthful readers of *Jack and Jill*: 'Our actions are in our own hands, but the consequences of them are not. Remember that . . . and think twice before you do anything.'[12]

Throughout the stories, the emphasis is on self-discipline, on the development of conscience and character—strong, reliable inner controls. Physical punishment is replaced by emotional manipulation, a pattern consistent with much child-rearing literature of the period. Stressing service and duty, the gentry sought to counter the narrowly economic definition of the self-made man. They held out the promise, in their fiction, that every American child could be a lady or a gentleman—in the essential matter of character—and that the benefits both to individuals and to American society would be great. Gentry authors took care, on occasion, to indicate that no barrier of class or regional origin stood in the way of the child who wished to be counted a gentleman or true lady. Education was the typical avenue to gentry status, but in the absence of formal schooling, a firm resolve to adhere to the Golden Rule—the quintessence of the gentry moral code—and unremitting self-culture were sufficient to permit accession to gentry status. A single story might be enough to stimulate the first step—the firm resolve to do better. And this belief about the efficacy of fiction was a powerful constraint shaping gentry literature for children.

A principal threat to the gentry concept of gentility was 'fashionability,' which fed on all that was showy, superficial, and external. Fashionability, embodied in a socioeconomic elite dedicated to exclusivity and conspicuous consumption but styling themselves ladies and gentlemen, represented a preoccupation with mere appearances that made a mockery of the essential link presumed to exist between character and manners. By its very nature, the spirit of fashion was compelled to seek out novel stimulation—a process that led inevitably, in the gentry view, to callousness and cynicism. Like alcohol, the spirit of fashion led to 'intolerable aberrations and illegalities.'[13] The gentry consistently portrayed fashionable society as enervated, superficial, parasitic—and unhealthy.

The city appeared to be another massive threat to gentry values, which were anchored in family life and rural settings. The city seemed inimical to the former and denied individuals close contact with the restorative influences of Nature. Artificial, noisy, and congested, urban life seemed antithetical to the most salient and valued characteristics of children. Nature symbolized moral law and exercised a beneficent discipline; the city, by contrast, symbolized aggressive competition, turmoil, and exploitation. 'Families run out in a generation or two of city life,' one gentry commentator warned, 'unless there is a constant, regular recourse to the country for more vitality.'[14]

As presented in the children's periodicals, the gentry ideal of character organized widely shared values in a distinctive way. More than an enumeration of appropriate traits such as courage, self-reliance, and social responsibility, the ideal defined a social identity, a concept of selfhood that was peculiarly adapted to the realities of American life and its promise. The gentleman and lady offered models for negotiating the difficult and precarious passage from childhood to adulthood as well as for moderating the economic competition between free men that was the most important social fact of American life in the nineteenth century. In addition, the gentry ideal represented a defensive stance appropriate to a fluid, precarious world; it offered the child an overarching definition of experience, in which she could interpret events and find meaning in pain and suffering. Throughout their fiction, the gentry authors defined misfortune both as test and opportunity. Adversity tested character or provided the occasion to learn that immutable moral law was at the heart of things. The world was best understood to be a school for character. The gentry ideal, then, was more than the social type most adapted to American social and political institutions; it reflected universal moral law, and its legitimacy ultimately rested on that close connection. Acceptance of the ideal promised to give meaning to suffering as well as to reduce the individual's vulnerability to the economic cycle of boom and bust, since character was not defined in monetary terms nor happiness in terms of elevated social position. Rather character and happiness were rooted in and expressed the individual's perception of universal moral principle.

If the historian is to specify the evidential significance of children's literature, he must reconstruct the factors which shaped that literature. The fiction in *St. Nicholas*, *Youth's Companion*, *Our Young Folks*, the *Riverside Magazine for Young People*, and *Wide Awake* was created by writers who identified with a distinctive group in American society, who had well-defined views concerning the nature of the child and the function of literature, who felt both threatened and exhilarated by the rapid economic expansion of the United States, and who found themselves engaged in economic and ideological competition with other elite groups in American society. Their fiction is evidence of the complex and subtle ways in which the gentry sought to create good literature for children and at the same time transmit the beliefs, values, and definitions that structured and gave meaning to their world.

The kind of analysis outlined here depends on certain sources, and I shall conclude by briefly noting these and stating what seem to me to be the implications for library acquisition. The principal source materials were, of course, the several children's periodicals already mentioned. These are relatively accessible, largely because the concept of literature which shaped them remains dominant in the field of children's literature. *St. Nicholas* is still regarded as the preeminent children's magazine produced in America. Less likely to be saved are the more obviously exploitative children's periodicals like *Frank Leslie's Boys' and Girls' Weekly* or the *Boys of New York*, which have not as yet been carefully studied. In addition to the children's periodicals, I drew on a wide range of materials—autobiographies, conduct books, editorial statements, and so forth. The logic of the approach suggested here implies that such materials, selected on the basis of the group producing them, ought to be considered integral to a research collection of children's literature. Additionally, manuscripts, when extant; an author's correspondence, especially with editors and publishers; and publishers' records, manuscript reports, and stipulations for revising manuscripts are important sources. In brief, it is necessary to know as much as possible about the processes which generate the documents to which the historian turns so that he can better estimate and specify what the documents are evidence of. In the case of literature generally, editorial changes are crucial factors to consider.

A final comment, then, on the matter of theory with which I began. To look at stories for children in the way that I have presupposes some assumptions—a minimal theory—about the relationships between literature, culture, and society. Had I assumed that literature was the product of inspired geniuses, working in isolation, who transcend their cultural milieus, I would have proceeded in a very different manner and reached very different conclusions. Meaning resides in context—and theory establishes the context for the historian's data.

🕇 🕇 🕇 🕇 🕇

PARTICIPANT: *You stressed* character *illumination. Yet in your tale of 'Nellie in the Light-house,' the child did figure out that pine knots did burn. Could you tell us what role was generally assigned in this particular genre to reason per se?*

KELLY: Well, I would stand by my earlier generalization, but add to my description of 'Nellie in the Light-house.' There is no suggestion given in the story that a reasoning process is involved at all. It is more a matter of an unexplained association, a recollection which lies, I think, so far as the story provides any evidence at all, outside any act of conscious reasoning. It is a kind of instinctive, but an *informed* instinctive response to the difficult situation in which Nellie finds herself, and I think it is important to note that it comes in that moment of calm which follows her memory of her mother's religious, and by definition, moral teaching. In general, I should say that reasoning is not given very much weight in these stories; what is desired is the kind of character that will respond instantaneously and almost with the force of instinct to the particular problem that the individual confronts, and I think that, recalling my reading of *A Moral Tale* (1975), this is pretty much what Anne MacLeod has concluded also. 'Book learning' is subordinated generally to the matter of moral character, and the two are distinguished from one another.

PARTICIPANT: *If you consider circulation figures for these magazines, do you find that they are representative of a kind of national consciousness, or are they more strictly regional?*

KELLY: Well, it is a fact that they do issue from Boston and New York—the ones I chose. Circulation figures are hard to obtain, and they are difficult to interpret when you do get them. The kinds of records we would like to have, which would allow graphing the geographical distribution of a magazine, for example, don't exist. There is a little evidence for calculating circulation in *St. Nicholas* and *Our Young Folks*, but not a great deal. First of all, there seems to have been, from around 1873 at least, a ceiling of perhaps seventy to eighty thousand circulation that *St. Nicholas* seldom seems to have gone above. *The Youth's Companion* had by far the greatest circulation of any periodical in the late nineteenth century, except for some mail-order catalogs, and was reaching five hundred thousand subscribers, and presumably more readers than that, by the turn of the century. The evidence from *Our Young Folks* and *St. Nicholas* suggests that there was a national distribution, but as we would expect, the subscribers were centered in New England, the Middle Atlantic states, and in the Midwest and the Old Northwest. Of course, that was where the population was also. The other half of your question, though, with respect to regionalism versus a national audience, I tried to deal with in terms of my sense of a group—the gentry elite, which had its publishing centers and its educational centers on the eastern seaboard, but was a national cultural elite. We would find people accepting the ideal of the gentleman and the lady throughout America. In that sense, it transcends the regional emphasis that I may have implied inadvertently.

PARTICIPANT: *Would you care to comment upon the frequent title change that took place within individual magazines and the reason behind it, if there was a reason?*

KELLY: This, I should think, is not characteristic of the magazines which I looked at, all of which, so far as I can recall, had but one title. *St. Nicholas* was always *St. Nicholas*; similarly, *The Youth's Companion* dropped a subtitle before I began looking at it, but remained *The Youth's Companion* throughout the period I was examining.

The analysis that I undertook was not designed to present change over time with regard to the values in the magazines; I did not use *Oliver Optic's Magazine*, for example. 'Optic' is one of the people that Anne MacLeod would consider a transition figure: different in kind and emphasis from the earlier nineteenth-century didactic writers. I would say he is not characteristic either of the values that you find in *St. Nicholas* and some of the other magazines I examined. He represents, I think, the beginnings of the kind of diversification in publication for children which occurs from the late 1840s on into the latter part of the century; at that time an increasingly divergent social source for people who are writing children's literature . . . people from quite different positions within American society than the group I have termed 'the gentry.' Louisa May Alcott objected on occasion to what she called the 'optical delusions,' of which Adams was guilty in her estimation; and similarly Alger. There is a considerable difference between the way Alger organizes his fiction and the way the 'gentry' organized theirs. They regarded Alger with ambivalence and a good deal of suspicion. They were not, in the end, ready to proscribe him, though there were some libraries in New England which did, in fact, take him off the shelves at one time or another; but they certainly viewed him with suspicion. I would not regard Alger, despite the fact that he came out of a New England Unitarian background, as being very near the center of what I would call the 'American gentry elite.' He exists, in fact, rather on the periphery of its value system.

PARTICIPANT: *What is the relationship between the periodical fiction that you examined and the period fiction in the form of novels?*

KELLY: It's characteristic of American publishing in this period that you often get the serialization of longer works of children's fiction in periodicals and then simultaneous or subsequent publication in book form. Aldrich's *Story of a Bad Boy* is one of these, and there are many others. The answer to this question lies in the extent to which my conclusions in *Mother Was a Lady* can be generalized to other materials. I would argue here that if you consider a writer like Howells or Aldrich, or some of the others who belonged to the cultural elite in the late nineteenth century, then these generalizations ought to hold for them because they were trying, in their literature, to do much the same thing. I did not look much at fiction that appeared outside the periodicals, but I would argue that literature issuing from this particular group during the period I examined is likely to be all of a piece, although there are surely variations from person to person. The social group, the gentry elite, while it has its base, and in a very real sense its home in New England especially, is by no means a narrowly provincial group. You see this, for example, in the distribution of responses in a contest which was held by *Our Young Folks* as to what constituted the 'true' gentleman and the 'true' lady. One year they offered to reward children with small amounts of money for their definition of what constituted gentility, and one of the winners was from Muscatine, Iowa, which was, at that time, a little river town upstream from Hannibal. And similarly, other responses came from Illinois and areas in the Midwest. But these were typically areas which were settled by descendants of New England and Middle Atlantic people.

PARTICIPANT: *Did you find certain set attitudes toward minority or new immigrants?*

KELLY: There are very few stories that I read that depict black children. Black adults tend to be depicted in the status of retainer, servants, and that kind of thing, but they are few and far between. As far as ethnic minorities—Irish, or new immigrants—there is very little of this, that I can recall. If you judge ethnicity on the basis of names ascribed to the characters, most of them are common English and Scottish names.

PARTICIPANT: *What was the importance for your research of publisher's correspondence?*

KELLY: I undertook no very systematic effort to identify where these sources existed. I examined the Lucy Larcom papers, which didn't prove very helpful. I decided not to quote from those letters, although some pertain to her editorship of *Our Young Folks*. I confess I didn't find it very helpful. I don't know whether the *St. Nicholas* editorial material exists or not. It would be useful—particularly as a kind of summary evidence of what it was the editors wanted. There are some editorial statements published late in the nineteenth century in *The Writer* magazine, and the editors of *Youth's Companion* contributed to the services. They stated the kinds of stories they were looking for; but one would like much more of this, and it would be nice to be able to see the letters which the editors addressed to authors, telling them to change this or that in the story or rejecting the manuscript because it didn't conform to certain editorial precepts. I have seen this kind of correspondence from the late editor of *Jack and Jill*, but I have not seen much otherwise.

PARTICIPANT: *With regard to the matter of discipline in the stories and the tendency to abandon physical punishment and replace it with some kind of emotional manipulation, did this consist of withdrawing love primarily?*

KELLY: The answer to that is 'yes.'

PARTICIPANT: *What was the relationship between British fiction, which might be considered to issue from a British gentry class, and its American counterpart?*

KELLY: I confess I know relatively little, unfortunately, about the British gentry literature, and there clearly was some; I suppose it is worth pointing out that *Little Lord Fauntleroy* represents, in my view, a very interesting bit of evidence along this line. Little Lord Fauntleroy, raised under the circumstances of American democracy, goes home to England in the end, and is rewarded with those ancestral estates and proceeds, presumably, to bring a higher sense of genteel obligation to the people who live on that estate than his English grandfather was providing. This suggests that from the American gentry point of view, the English gentry had fallen away from their responsibilities perhaps, and needed a good dose of American egalitarian society, in childhood's formative years, for the balance to be restored back home. Beyond that, I don't think I would want to comment on the relationship except that recently it has been argued, and I think the evidence is overwhelming, that there is a clear tie between the spokesmen of Victorian England and the version of Victorianism that we had. There is a good deal of overlap in their views. There is much correspondence among the leading spokesmen, and one would expect to find similar views about the importance of character, for example, but I would think that in Britain you would find a good deal of class consciousness that would be anathema to American gentry spokesmen.

PARTICIPANT: *How many British writers essentially were contributing to American children's periodicals of the kind you discussed?*

KELLY: I didn't undertake to identify writers on the basis of nationality. There are English writers who contributed to American periodicals—Jean Ingelow, a well-known British Victorian writer, was one of these. On the whole, the nationalism that engendered American children's fiction before the Civil War was very much a part of it afterwards; and what was desired and published, on the whole, were stories which would be American stories for American children, and which would eliminate the class consciousness, or play down the class biases, which the American gentry saw even in the late nineteenth century as being typical of British fiction. *Tom Brown's Schooldays*, for all its similarities to later school sports stories in this country, still has very clear evidences of its British class origins in it. Ingelow's stories, and a poem of hers that I recall, were unobjectionable on this score.

PARTICIPANT: *Do you think that the publication of* Alice in Wonderland *had any influence on periodical fiction of the time?*

KELLY: I don't know. This is very different kind of literature, after all, from the kind of didactic stories I was examining. I don't see that it influenced the gentry's narrative fiction, but I confess I was not looking for and may not have been alert to obvious influences that you may find there.

PARTICIPANT: *Is there any indication of the literature's effect upon its readers as seen, perhaps, in letters to the editor?*

KELLY: I was convinced that such evidence is very difficult to deal with, and so I indulged myself by ignoring that whole issue, preferring to speculate, hopefully, on somewhat better ground, about the relationship between the adult producers and the fiction that they wrote. There are anecdotal kinds of evidence, and certainly that would be one thing to consider. There are references, for example, in Theodore Roosevelt's papers to the importance of *Our Young Folks* at a formative period in his life. He testifies to the influence of the ideals in *Our Young Folks*, but it is difficult to know what to make of that kind of evidence on the basis of these references. John Morton Blum, a Yale historian, looked at *Our Young Folks* and wrote an interesting essay about its values and ideals, but steered clear of the question as to how these might have really influenced Roosevelt except to point out that there were certain obvious parallels between certain aspects of progressive thought and some of the values and ideas that you find in the periodical. It's a recalcitrant problem; it is not one which I think is easily solved despite Thoreau's statement to the effect—who cannot recall having his life changed by a book.

PARTICIPANT: *Did you see some response in the periodical literature to the growing militarism in American society in the late nineteenth century?*

KELLY: I confess that again I can recall very few such stories. A few deal with the Civil War, although these are rare. I think that the same pattern that Anne MacLeod found obtains in this literature as well. The authors weren't, I suspect, pacifists, but they certainly didn't glorify war; moreover, they did not want to encourage children to go off adventuring—to regard war as a lark. In one story that I recall, a boy pleads with his mother to let him go off to the Civil War. He is fourteen or so. She reluctantly lets him go. He serves as a drummer, not as a combatant. It is generally characteristic of this fiction that aggression and violence are not regarded as appropriate solutions to problems—war included. You find very little emphasis on violent solutions. And when you do get competition (to respond to a question that was raised concerning Anne MacLeod's paper), in the late nineteenth century, it is in the form of prep school athletic rivalry, whose heroes are Dink Stover or Frank Merriwell. That marks, in my mind, a decisive change in the organization of the values which are being mediated to children for emulation and represents the abandonment, to a considerable extent, of the traditional gentry character that obtains in these magazines up through the late nineteenth century.

NOTES

1. Bernard Wishy, *The Child and the Republic* (Philadelphia: University of Pennsylvania Press, 1968). *American Historical Review*, 81(1976):211–12.

2. R. Gordon Kelly, 'Literature and the Historian,' *American Quarterly*, 26(1974): 141–59.

3. Stow Persons, *The Decline of American Gentility* (New York: Columbia University Press, 1973).

4. John G. Cawelti, *Adventure, Mystery and Romance* (Chicago: University of Chicago Press, 1976).

5. James Spradley, ed., *Culture and Cognition* (San Francisco: Chandler, 1972), p. 21.

6. Peter Berger and Thomas Luckmann, *The Social Construction of Reality* (Garden City, New York: Doubleday, 1966).

7. Kenneth Burke, *The Philosophy of Literary Form*, revised edition, abridged by the author (New York: Vintage Books, 1957), p. 3.

8. Susan Archer Weiss, 'Nellie in the Light-house,' *St. Nicholas*, 4(1877):577–80.

9. Clarence Gordon ['Vieux Moustache,' Pseud.], 'Charlie Balch's Metamorphosis,' *Riverside Magazine for Young People*, 1(1867):106–12.

10. Ibid., p. 110.

11. Quoted in R. Gordon Kelly, *Mother Was a Lady* (Westport, Ct.: Greenwood Press, 1974), p. 32.

12. 'Jack and Jill,' *St. Nicholas*, 7(1879):387.

13. George Henry Calvert, *The Gentleman* (Boston: Ticknor and Fields, 1863), pp. 129–30.

14. 'Accomplished Gentlemen,' *Overland Monthly*, n.s. 6(1885):207.

4.
REGIONALISM IN AMERICAN CHILDREN'S LITERATURE

FRED ERISMAN

Ideas are not spontaneous. They do not emerge from nothing, fearful in their symmetry and immaculate in their conception. Instead, like biological organisms, they evolve. They have parents and grandparents, ancestors and antecedents, and carry with them the traces of their inheritance. In their heredity lies their value to the student of social history, for within the confines of any specific idea can be found evidences of its development—the dominant and recessive genes deeded it by its forebears, the scars acquired in its own lifetime, the vitality that can influence its future. An idea is a living entity. It comes from somewhere; it goes somewhere. For the student of history, it provides a guide to the world from which it has come, and a means by which one can glimpse the world into which it is going.

A clear-cut demonstration of the evolution of ideas occurs in the course of the development of American regional juvenile literature. Like a maturing organism, the genre recapitulates the phylogeny of its kind. It reflects the forms of the parent literature, sharing all of the strengths and the weaknesses that the other possesses. Thus, juvenile regionalism, like adult regionalism, has its beginnings in the local-color story, presenting a sentimentalized view of the far-flung diversity of the United States. Gaining complexity in the later nineteenth century, in the twentieth century it comes into its own, emerging from the works of a number of writers as a full-fledged regional literature, in which place, story, and character are tightly integrated. This integration, which reveals the complex involvement of human, cultural, and geographical influences, produces a rich literature—peculiarly rich for the student of American culture, and extraordinarily rich for the young persons fortunate enough to read it.

One of the most significant literary developments of the post-Civil War years in the United States was the appearance of the local-color story. The war, with its far-ranging campaigns and its emphasis upon transportation, had understandably increased the sectional awareness of the American people. Numerous authors, among them Bret Harte, George Washington Cable, and Joel

55

Chandler Harris, took note of this awareness. In works such as Harte's 'The Luck of Roaring Camp' (1868), Cable's *Old Creole Days* (1879), and Harris's *Uncle Remus, His Songs and His Sayings* (1881) they combined the romantic flair and sentimental tones of earlier works of popular fiction with the newly-found picturesque and indigenous in American life, creating the first notable acknowledgment of America's cultural diversity in the nineteenth century.[1]

These works achieved two historically significant ends. First, by exending the well-established traditions of the nineteenth-century sentimental novel, they helped to perpetuate a simplistic, even naive view of human life. Moreover, by applying these same sentimental traditions to the diverse regions of the United States, the stories helped to reunite the divided nation. As their authors wrote of the shared beliefs and feelings that lay beneath the surface differences of the residents of varied locales, they dramatized the emotional cohesiveness of American life, even as they emphasized the variety of the American setting.[2]

Not surprisingly, the authors of juvenile works soon followed suit, producing for their readers books embodying the same attributes found in local-color stories written for an adult audience. Noah Brooks's *The Boy Emigrants* (1877) takes its young heroes through the expanses of the Great Plains. Kate Douglas Wiggin's *A Summer in a Cañon* (1889) tells of a pastoral camping trip in the California countryside, complete with Chinese cook and Mexican handymen. Edward Eggleston's *The Hoosier School-Boy* (1883) reconstructs boyhood days in rural Ohio, while Thomas Bailey Aldrich's *The Story of a Bad Boy* (1870) gives glimpses of life in a New England seafaring town. In each of these, as in the adult stories, the plots are familiar—comic pranks, sentimental quests, transient quarrels, and the like, acted out before the backdrop of a particular place. In portraying that place, however, the authors attempt in several ways to convey a sense of the particular and varied locality in which the events occur.

One way in which the writers create a sense of a particular location is through the reproduction of indigenous dialects. By stressing the particular and the peculiar in the speech of a region's

people, the local colorist can easily create a sense of local unique-
ness.[3] Thus, for example, Sarah Orne Jewett economically makes
a number of points about New England ways when one of her
goodwives remarks to Betty Leicester, 'Oh, bless ye! when it
comes to seafarin' I'm right to home, I tell you. I didn't know but
you'd had to come from some o' them Londons out West; all the
way by cars. I've got a sister that lives to London, Iowy; she comes
East every three or four year; passes two days an' two nights,
I believe 't is, on the cars; makes nothin' of it. I ain't been so great
of a traveler. Creation's real queer, *ain't* it!'[4] In much the same
way, on the other side of the continent, Kate Douglas Wiggin
communicates a part of California culture as her Polly Oliver
attempts to teach a Chinese cook some English: 'As no Chinaman
can pronounce the letter "r," . . . when she attempted to introduce the sentence, "Around the rough and rugged rock the ragged
rascal ran," Hop Yet rose hurriedly, remarking, "All lightee: I go
no more school jus' now. I lun get lunchee." '[5] Language, clearly,
conveys local differences.

A more striking way in which local colorists present sectional
differences is by the use of idiosyncratic, localized character
types. These persons, often rural and always picturesque, constitute the quintessence of provincial character.[6] They may be
garrulous back-country yarnspinners, as is Simon Wheeler in
Mark Twain's 'Jumping Frog of Calaveras County,' or benign
advisors and counselors of the young, as is Joel Chandler Harris's
Uncle Remus. Whatever their form, however, they are persons
growing out of the locale, their attitudes and behavior powerfully
influenced by the time and place in which they live.[7]

Such a one is Uncle Jerry Cobb, the stage-driver in Kate Douglas
Wiggin's *Rebecca of Sunnybrook Farm* (1903). Unschooled and
rustic though he is, his knowledge of Maine folkways and village
tensions enables him to guide Rebecca through one crisis after
another. When Rebecca, spiritually bruised by an undeserved
scolding from her Aunt Miranda, runs away, it is Uncle Jerry who
puts the matter into perspective: 'Now ain't it too bad you've jest
got to give it all up on account o' your Aunt Mirandy? Well, I
can't hardly blame ye. She's cranky an' she's sour; I should think
she'd ben nussed on bonny-clabber an' green apples. She needs

bearin' with; an' I guess you ain't much on patience, be ye . . . ?
She's turrible hard to get along with, an' kind o' heaves benefits at
your head, same's she would bricks; but they're benefits jest the
same, an' mebbe it's your job to kind o' pay for 'em in good
behavior.'[8] By his astute reading of Miranda's character, Uncle
Jerry opens Rebecca's eyes to a part of human life and responsibility previously unknown to her.

Of all the techniques of the local colorists, the most striking is
the conscious use of a specific, particularized setting. Although
the setting in a local-color story serves as little more than a stage
for the action of the story, it nonetheless helps to contribute to
the atmosphere of the events that the story relates.[9] Thus, the
Mississippi River is an important part of Mark Twain's *Huckleberry Finn* (1885), and the Southwestern landscape adds appeal
to Frances Courtenay Baylor's *Juan and Juanita* (1888). In like
fashion, Thomas Bailey Aldrich gives a memorable picture of the
sea and its influence as he writes:

> Every Rivermouth boy looks upon the sea as being in some way
> mixed up with his destiny. . . . The gables and roofs of the houses
> facing eastward are covered with red rust, like the flukes of old
> anchors; a salty smell pervades the air, and dense gray fogs, the
> very breath of Ocean, periodically creep up into the quiet streets
> and envelop everything. The terrific storms that lash the coast; the
> kelp and spars, and sometimes the bodies of drowned men, tossed
> on shore by the scornful waves . . . these things, and a hundred
> other, feed the imagination and fill the brain of every healthy boy
> with dreams of adventure.[10]

No person, even one from the arid plains, can fail to carry away
from this passage a New Englander's sense of the sea.

The same sense of a particular place and its special perils
appears in L. Frank Baum's *The Wonderful Wizard of Oz* (1900).
The place of which Baum writes is a nineteenth-century Kansas
farm, but his description of the locale is as evocative as Aldrich's:

> When Dorothy stood in the doorway and looked around, she

could see nothing but the great gray prairie on every side. Not a tree nor a house broke the broad sweep of flat country that reached to the edge of the sky in all directions. The sun had baked the plowed land into a gray mass, with little cracks running through it. Even the grass was not green, for the sun had burned the tops of the long blades until they were the same gray color to be seen everywhere. Once the house had been painted, but the sun blistered the paint and the rains washed it away, and now the house was as dull and gray as everything else.[11]

Where Aldrich uses the locale to set a note of adventure, however, Baum uses it to create an atmosphere of Midwestern sterility and drought that makes all the more dramatic the luxuriant beauty of the Land of Oz.

For all their differences, these works, and others like them, share two qualities. First, they present to American children a realistic picture of the variety of the United States. It is a country of fog-ridden seacoast towns, fertile valleys, and desiccated plains; it is a country of blacks and whites, of yellow and brown; it is a country with a single tongue, albeit one spoken in myriad accents. It is, in sum, a diverse and enormously varied nation. With this conclusion no one can quarrel. Second, however, the stories convey a sentimentalized view of human life. Despite the stories' surface reality in language and setting, their young readers encounter in them citizens of a country notably different from that in which the tales are being told. Far from being representative of modern types, these characters are often carry-overs from an earlier age, persons whose thoughts reflect the ideals of a pre-industrial, apolitical, largely rural America.[12] So even as the stories acquaint their readers with new locales, they transmit the attitudes of an earlier time. The result, whether accidental or intended, is to pass on to the members of the next generation a conservative, traditional view of American life.

If the local-color story is characteristically nineteenth-century in its origins, the truly regional work is a product of the twentieth century. Building upon its forebears, assimilating the homely realism of the sentimental novel and the vivid particularity of the local-color tale, it mutates, modifies, and evolves, becoming a totally new kind of literature. At least two influences contribute to the coming of this genre. The first is plainly the nation's growing sense of its involvement with the rest of the world; by 1918, the United States had been a world power with extensive international commitments for a quarter of a century.[13] The second, which can perhaps be traced from the Centennial observances of 1876, is a new sense of American history. The United States in the twentieth century was no longer a young, emerging nation. It was an established power, with its own unique history, and its own unique responsibilities.

A people's sense of history, Lewis Mumford writes, leads to a regional vision through a predictable sequence. There is, he says, 'at first a poetic cycle: this is the recovery of the language and literature of the folk, and the attempt to use it as a vehicle of expression, on the basis of traditional forms.' This, obviously, is analogous to the development of American local-color writing. 'The second,' he continues, 'is the cycle of prose, in which the interest in the language leads to an interest in the totality of a community's life and history, and so brings the movement on to the contemporary stage; and finally, there is the cycle of action, in which regionalism forms for itself a fresh objective, political, economic, civic, on the basis of its growing integration.'[14] Society's attention, in short, moves from concentrating upon the purely local to a broader integration of the total regional experience. American literature, adult and juvenile, does the same.

When expressed in literature, regionalism requires three necessary conditions. The first 'is that the region must enter constructively into the story, as another character, as the instigator of plot.' Second, the regional story 'must not only be about the country, it must be of it . . . , taking its movement and rhythm, its structure and intention, or lack of it, from the scene . . . reflecting in some fashion the essential qualities of the land.'[15] Third, and finally, the regional work must, as Mumford makes clear, place the setting and the story 'on to the contemporary stage,' giving to the reader the sense that the events being related are a part of the 0greater sweep of human history. Thus, for example, O. E. Rolvaag's *Giants in the Earth* (1927) tells of pioneering hardships in the Great Plains, but also involves national rivalries and individual guilt. Jack Schaefer's *Shane* (1949) is in one sense merely another gunfighter novel with a picturesque setting, yet in a greater sense speaks to the whole range of individual hope, duty, and love. And Harper Lee's *To Kill a Mockingbird* (1960), though certainly telling the story of personal and racial tensions in a small Southern town, embeds these tensions in the context of the world as it relates them to the Great Depression and the rise of Nazi Germany.

American juvenile literature of the twentieth century contains some distinguished examples of genuinely regional writing. These include, as representatives of one expression of regionalism, the 'Little House' books of Laura Ingalls Wilder (1932 on) and Marjorie Kinnan Rawlings's *The Yearling* (1938); more recently, there are Vera and Bill Cleaver's *Where the Lilies Bloom* (1969) and Laurence Yep's *Dragonwings* (1975). In these works, the regional presence is strong. There is the requisite sense of place— place as a part of the plot, and not just a backdrop. 'The great, dark trees of the Big Woods stood all around . . . ,' Mrs. Wilder writes, 'and beyond them were more trees. As far as a man could go to the north in a day, or a week, or a whole month, there was nothing but woods. There were no houses. There were no roads. There were no people. There were only trees and the wild animals who had their homes among them.'[16] She does not need to add that she is going to tell of the self-sufficiency of the Ingalls family; the setting does it for her. In the later books of the series, the varied settings have a continuing impact upon the family's fortunes. Thus, the isolation of Wisconsin is intensified when the family moves to the Indian Territory, and realizes the remoteness of friends and family. When they move to Minnesota, Pa's small-scale garden becomes a large-scale wheat field with prospects of money and security, but their hopes are dashed as a swarm of grasshoppers devastates the crop.[17] Each region, with its particular traits, becomes an integral element of the plot.

The same sense emerges from *The Yearling*, as Mrs. Rawlings describes life in the Florida scrub forests. The conflicts of the Baxter family are accentuated by their isolation and their enforced closeness with the natural world. Water and food have to be scrabbled from the environment; goods such as powder, shot, thread, and coffee are to be had only after a protracted journey, and the family is accustomed to doing without them for long periods. But, despite the physical hardships that the setting forces upon them, the Baxters derive from their isolation a peculiar comfort. Of Penny Baxter Mrs. Rawlings writes:

> The peace of the vast aloof scrub had drawn him with the beneficence of its silence. Something in him was raw and tender. The touch of men was hurtful upon it, but the touch of the pines was healing. Making a living came harder there, distances were troublesome in the buying of supplies and the marketing of crops. But the clearing was peculiarly his own. The wild animals seemed less predatory to him than people he had known. The forays of bear and wolf and wildcat and panther on stock were understandable, which was more than he could say of human cruelties.[18]

From Penny's personal seeking of an isolated comfort comes the more general geographical situation that affects the book's themes.

These juvenile works also reflect the adjustment that individuals must make to the land, accepting its movement and rhythm and adapting their own processes of life to it. Far from civilization in the Indian Territory, for example, the Ingalls family adapts a homely legend to suit geographical and climatic circumstances: ' "Didn't he have his reindeer?" Laura asked. "You know he couldn't," Mary said. "There isn't any snow." "Exactly," said Mr. Edwards. "Santa Claus traveled with a pack-mule in the southwest." '[19] The hand-to-mouth existence of the Baxter family compels them into set patterns of living. Crops must be tended, yet time must be found in which to hunt for meat; a drawn-out hunt, such as that for the rogue bear, Old Slewfoot, means time unavoidably taken from family routine, and the final conflict of the book emerges from the family's inability to retain a pet that threatens their crops.[20] Here, too, the nature of the place exerts a powerfully determining influence upon the way life is lived.

In these works appears, finally, the awareness that a world exists outside of the immediate confines of the particular setting, a contemporary world with its own ways and values that inexorably affects the life of every individual. In the 'Little House' books, young Almanzo Wilder gets an enduring lesson in practical capitalism during a Fourth of July celebration; the Ingalls family is ousted from their Indian Territory homestead by a governmental decision made two thousand miles away; and their growing dependence upon the railroad and the goods that it brings from outside their region dawns vividly when the Long Winter seals them into De Smet.[21] A world of another sort opens up to Jody Baxter in the course of *The Yearling*, as he glimpses exotic scenes and adult rivalries through the seafaring Oliver Hutto, and as, at the end of the novel, he confronts his childhood's passing. Accepting his father's weakness, his mother's grim realism, and the death of his pet deer, he faces up to manhood: 'He would be lonely all his life. But a man took it for his share and went on. . . . Somewhere beyond the sinkhole, past the magnolia, under the live oaks, a boy and a yearling ran side by side, and were gone forever.'[22] In each case, the young characters become increasingly aware of the larger world and its responsibilities, and incorporate this knowledge into their lives.

The Yearling and the 'Little House' books are rural stories, as might be expected; regionalism is often equated with ruralism. The same attributes of regionalism, however, also appear in works with urban settings. These works Blanche Gelfant has characterized as 'ecological novels,' which provide 'a detailed exploration of the manners and morals of a cohesive group of city people . . . [and] a minute and comprehensive portrayal of how urban people think, act, and feel. The reader comes to understand the inner life of a community in terms of the perceptions of its people.'[23] Typical of these works are Waldo Frank's *City Block* (1922) and Willard Motley's *Knock on Any Door* (1947). The ecological novel appears in juvenile literature as well as in adult literature. In one notable instance, the city is New York; the group is the Melendy family; and the book is Elizabeth Enright's *The Saturdays* (1941). Here, in a work with an urban setting, Miss Enright provides an eminently regional story.

The Saturdays satisfies each of the three requirements of regional literature. The diverse offerings of New York, which Miss Enright knows from her own childhood, provide the impetus for the plot, as the four Melendy children seek a way to fill in idle, urban Saturdays.[24] In addition, the setting is totally a part of the characters' lives. The city provides the Metropolitan Opera and Carnegie Hall to satisfy young Rush's yearning for Bach and Wagner; it provides Madison Square Garden to satisfy six-year-old Oliver's hankering for the circus; and it provides art galleries to exhibit the French Impressionist paintings that so deeply move Miranda.[25] The Melendys are children, to be sure, but they are also urban children, accustomed to adapting their lives and activities to what the city offers. The reader sees them as persons, and he sees how the city has made its mark upon them.

Even as *The Saturdays* delineates the city as ecosphere, it supplies a sense of the world outside of the city. The Melendy children know that their well-being depends upon their father's maintaining his competence as an economist, and they tolerate his frequent absences on professional duties. They learn, through their elderly friend Mrs. Oliphant, of the remorseless coming of old age, and its consequences. And they learn, indeed are constantly aware, that the world is at war. Their father warns them against a too-idealized view of mankind, remarking that 'Sometimes I think the Golden Age must have been the Age of Reptiles,' and the well-lighted New York skyline reminds them that Europe under the Blitz is another world indeed.[26] The book, in short, is all that a regional novel ought to be. Drawing upon her own consciousness of the complex contradictions of the present, Miss Enright gives to her readers the same sense of place and time that the authors of more rural works give, but does so within the boundaries of the contemporary city and the contemporary world.

Regionalism in American children's literature develops in distinct stages, originating in the early nineteenth century and maturing in the mid-twentieth century. As it progresses through these stages, it reveals a threefold consistency of pattern and theme. One finds in it, as in the adult works that it parallels, an increasingly keen sense of local distinctiveness: the authors of the times attempt to dramatize the qualities that identify each locale. Moreover, as the culture from which it arises becomes more sophisticated, the literature reflects that culture's growing awareness of its ties with its times and with the world at large. Finally, and most generally, it tends to perpetuate several persistent American national myths.

One of the most enduring of these national myths is that of the rural ideal. As Yi-Fu Tuan, a social geographer, points out, 'The dominant myths of America are nonurban. . . . The dominant spatial metaphors for American destiny, particularly in the nineteenth century, are the garden, the West, the frontier, and wilderness. The city, by contrast, stands for the world's temptations and iniquities.'[27] Thus, Kate Douglas Wiggin's California youngsters turn from the city to the pleasures of the Cañon Las Flores. Sarah Orne Jewett's Betty Leicester finds in rural Maine what she has longed for in urban Europe. Marjorie Kinnan Rawlings's Jody Baxter learns that life in the Florida scrub brings maturity as surely as does running away to sea. Frank Baum's Oz, for all of its magical overtones, is still an agrarian state; only in the last two or three of the 'Little House' books does anything resembling an urban society begin to appear; and even the thoroughly urbanized Melendy family moves at last to the rural calm of the Four-Story Mistake. The countryside retains its attractiveness, even into the urbanized present.

A second, equally enduring belief that runs throughout these works is the conviction that the world has direction, and certainty, and meaning. There are, of course, setbacks—some minor, some tragic—but the general tendency of life is toward the better. Thus, Mona Melendy meets paternal wrath when she first cuts her hair and blossoms forth with nail polish, but from the wrath comes a new understanding for father and daughter alike. The rigors of the Long Winter give the Ingalls family a greater appreciation of familial and social interdependence, and the death of Fodder-Wing Forrester creates one of the first breaks in the animosity between the Forresters and the Baxters.[28] Unity with the external world provides unity with the internal world as well.

The mythic persistence of the American belief in unity and balance is undeniable. It is implicit in the Founding Fathers' intention to create 'a more perfect union.' It arises in more elaborate form in Ralph Waldo Emerson's contention that 'the sure years reveal the deep remedial force that underlies all new facts,' for life invariably 'permits or constrains the formation of new acquaintances and the reception of new influences that prove of the first importance to the next years; and the man or woman who would have remained a sunny garden-flower . . . by the falling of the walls and the neglect of the gardener is made the banian of the forest, yielding shade and fruit to wide neighborhoods of men.'[29] And it is, finally, linked with locale by Eudora Welty, who notes that 'it is through place that we put out roots, wherever birth, chance, fate, or our traveling selves set us down; but where those roots reach toward . . . is the deep and running vein, eternal and consistent and everywhere purely itself—that feeds and is fed by the human understanding.'[30] The American accepts life wholly, confident of its coherence and consistency.

The persistence of these myths in American juvenile regional literature justifies the social historian's concern with the genre, for the persistence, while puzzling, is revealing. At a time when American society is undergoing rapid and profound changes, when the role of the individual and the family is increasingly being questioned, and when the role of the nation itself in world affairs is becoming increasingly ambivalent, a major component of American juvenile literature continues to espouse myths from the nation's past.[31] In this espousal of antiquated myths can certainly be seen a reluctance to confront reality; indeed, more than one critic has made that very argument.[32] To the historian, however, the continuum of local characteristics and national myths suggests something far more significant: that American authors, in giving their young readers the past and the present, attempt to give them the future.

Basic to the American character is change. From the very outset, the United States has stressed its mobility and its newness, deriving 'its character precisely from its social impermanence, from its shifting (which is, in the broad sense, to say *frontier*) characteristics.'[33] Thus, Holgrave, the daguerreotypist in *The House of the Seven Gables*, is a vehement spokesman for impermanence, and one of Henry James's most memorable protagonists is the American, Christopher Newman. Change and the quest for newness permeate American life, past and present. The quest, however, has its price, for as the pace of life increases, so does the pace of change, until Americans at last are confronted with a life 'so ephemeral, unfamiliar and complex as to threaten millions with adaptive breakdown' in their dealings with it. 'This breakdown,' Alvin Toffler goes on to say, 'is future shock.'[34]

In diagnosing future shock, Toffler also prescribes a cure. 'To manage change,' he writes, 'we must anticipate it. . . . We *can* assign probabilities to some of the changes that lie in store for us, especially certain large structural changes, and there are ways to use this knowledge in designing personal stability zones.' These zones he defines as 'certain enduring relationships that are carefully maintained despite all kinds of other changes.'[35] Thus, by creating areas of lasting consistency that are peculiarly his own, the individual is able to endure the flux that surrounds him. Toffler announced his diagnosis and his prescription in 1970. The authors of American regional fiction for children anticipated his conclusions by almost a century.

The consistency of attitudes within American regional juvenile fiction is the literary equivalent of Toffler's prescription for the chaos of the present. By demonstrating the ways in which diverse persons have effectively come to terms with their place and their time, the literature suggests to the young reader that he, too, can create a zone of stability, a personal frame of reference within which he is proof against the present and against which he can test its blandishments. 'It is by knowing where you stand that you grow able to judge where you are,' Eudora Welty writes. 'Place . . . bestows on us our original awareness; and our critical powers spring up from the study of it and the growth of experience inside it. . . . One place comprehended can make us understand other places better. Sense of place gives equilibrium; extended, it is sense of direction too.'[36] In the American's past, his present, and his place lies his future.

In the persistent continuity of these ideas is the historical importance of regional literature for young persons, for through the literature the present attempts to advise the future. The literature, to be sure, reinforces the American commitment to change, adapting it only slightly into the lasting conviction that the future can—and likely will—be better. But, at the very time that it advocates a generalized change, it equips the individual to tolerate that change, showing how each generation has accepted change within the greater context of life, both local and national, demonstrating the verities that retain their value whatever their surroundings.

The regional work, with its continuity of human relationships, helps its young reader to see where he is and where he has been. As it does so, it fits him to see where he is going, for it helps him to establish the personal stability that makes him a balanced individual. By enabling him to measure himself against the universal concerns of all mankind, the literature leads the reader to see himself as individual but not alone; a citizen of the section, the nation, and the world; a person capable of living tranquilly in the chaotic world of the present, capable in time of creating that more perfect union of the Founding Fathers' dream.

🛉 🛉 🛉 🛉 🛉

PARTICIPANT: *Since regionalism seems to depend so much on a specific language, does then regional literature depend also upon a lower middle or lower class sociological group?*

ERISMAN: I think not, for at least two reasons. First of all, we find the burden placed upon language primarily in the local-color writings, so that there the language itself carries far more of the story than anything else. What would Uncle Remus be in basic English? On the other hand, in the regional work, as I define it, language is only a part of a much greater picturing of the world, so that while we certainly can find lower-middle-class life in something like *Where the Lilies Bloom*, I argue that we also find it in upper-middle-class life as in the Melendys. It is the totality of the picture that is given that, to me, constitutes regionalism, and the awareness that out there is a limited world that exerts its influence upon us. One of the continuing problems that I am working with, not just in juvenile literature, but in other literature, is what happens to the regional experience in an increasingly urbanized mass culture world? Don't ask me to answer that question. Ask me in ten years.

PARTICIPANT: *In American picture books far beyond the time span of your talk, there has been a history of individuals yearning to get away from the city and back to the country. Would you care to comment?*

ERISMAN: This, as I see it, is a manifestation, an expression, of one of the enduring strains in American life—not the rural strain, but the romantic strain. If you read carefully some of the writings of the nature writers today, you see that what they have to say is little more than warmed-over Transcendentalism.

PARTICIPANT: *You didn't mention Lois Lenski.*

ERISMAN: I omitted her deliberately because she is too easy for my purposes. In her regional work such as *Cotton in My Sack, Judy's Journey, Bayou Suzette*, she deliberately sets out to reconstruct a particular culture. Do you know her Newbery Award speech? It's fascinating reading, for in the speech she talks of what she is trying to do in writing the regional series. When did she win the Newbery? A long time ago—1946—thirty years ago. She had a sense that it was important for American young people to know that there were subcultures around the country, each one affected by ethnic backgrounds, geographic backgrounds, economic backgrounds. This comes back to the question about economics as well. As I remember the ones of her works I have read, she goes all the way from settlement-house youngsters to fairly well-off Amish farmers in the course of the series. So I left Lois Lenski out on purpose.

PARTICIPANT: *There seems to be a trend in modern children's literature to have an urban setting, and we're not getting many books with a story set in the Midwest.*

ERISMAN: John Rowe Townsend a couple of years ago wrote an article in *Horn Book* titled 'The Now Child.' This article, I think, speaks to your question. He sees this phenomenon as the result of the publisher's jumping on the bandwagon to publish something 'relevant,' an irrelevant theme being one that doesn't deal with the city, or the ghetto. I think this possibly has something to do with it. I personally deplore this publishing fad.

PARTICIPANT: *Since seventy percent of the population now lives in urban centers, the publishers are going to slant their products toward the self-image of the public.*

PARTICIPANT: *Is the nostalgia craze going to affect juvenile writing to a re-creation of an earlier, calmer time?*

ERISMAN: Well, I was arguing here that juvenile literature follows adult literary trends like the Constitution follows the flag, and since we see a novel like E. L. Doctorow's *Ragtime*, with its very careful reconstruction of an era, climbing up the best-seller charts, it may. More to the point, the television popularity of 'The Waltons' or 'Little House on the Prairie'—(God forbid)—also in a way speaks to it. The United States basically is a highly romantic country, and we are living in a highly romantic age (that is, 'Romantic' with a capital 'R'). Anything is possible; I'm not fencing with you; I'm trying to resist it.

PARTICIPANT: *Has the American myth of the superiority of rural life begun to crumble because there are persons who simply prefer to live in the city (and raise families)?*

ERISMAN: Quite obviously it has. Truth—this is the beauty of dealing with myth—doesn't matter. It's what you think that counts. We are living and writing and reading in the very curious (for the historian) situation of seeing one thing all about us (certainly you can live a perfectly sound, happy, wholesome life in the city), and yet are being led to believe another. This can lead to all kinds of complications. To that extent, yes, I think the myth has crumbled a little bit, but we still cling to it. My quarrel with the city stories is not because they are city stories, but because they are pushing a highly slanted view of city life. This is the same kind of point Townsend makes. I think that a fine, fine piece of work could be done writing about city life as city life. I would love to see it. It is long overdue. There is nothing wrong with accepting the ugly side of the city. It is there; just walk down the street and you'll see it. But there is a lot else that is present, too. Some of Mary Rodgers's work, in something like *Freaky Friday*, comes close to it. *Harriet the Spy* is another possibility. The last word hasn't been said.

PARTICIPANT: *Has the world, as presented by Disney—the Disney version—perhaps affected our view, not just because so much of the Disney films are rural, but because they are small town?*

ERISMAN: Oddly enough, the Disney films that are truly citified, generally are distinctly inferior. This may have something to do with it.

PARTICIPANT: *What about science fiction and fantasy? Where does that fit in this scheme?*

ERISMAN: There are several ways to respond. Let me suggest two of them. One is that in much of science fiction and fantasy, the issues are fairly clear-cut, and so the children can turn away from the ambiguity that they see all around them and turn to a world where things are at least a little clearer. That is one way of looking at it. It is questionable, but I have heard it advanced, and I think there is some merit to it. A second interpretation ties into something a little more complex, the 'Turner Hypothesis of American Life,' arguing that life in the United States was made peculiar and unique throughout a good part of the formative years by the existence of a Frontier, so that the malcontent in the East could always go out to the Appalachians, cross the Frontier, and start over. Frederick Jackson Turner noted in 1890 that the Frontier was proclaimed closed, and so in 1893 raised the question, 'What's going to happen now?' Possibly, we see in the increasing popularity of good-quality science fiction and fantasy a way of creating our own frontier. If we can't cross it figuratively (we can't all be astronauts), we can cross it mentally; it's a way out, quite literally.

PARTICIPANT: *Is not science fiction and fantasy a way of coming to grips with questions that cannot satisfactorily be answered by a young reader in this world? The decisions are easier to make; the conclusions are easier to reach, you suggest, because these take place in another world and in another context.*

ERISMAN: Could be. It's easier to think abstractly about something that doesn't affect you individually, and we can think about flooding the canals of Mars when we might not want to think about ecology and water conservation here. That's a good idea.

PARTICIPANT: *Is it not that science fiction deals with the individual against an oppressive society in so many of its works and also that particularly during the decade of the fifties, it was chiefly the only free literature? Is that fair to say?*

ERISMAN: Yes, that is part of it. We must not overlook that science fiction is the only literary genre that consistently from its very inception has been fronting directly the whole problem of a technological society. It has a headstart on all of us. So when you go back to the thirties, you find writers like John Campbell who have been writing space fiction about problems that today we are right up against: poisoned atmosphere and so on. Isaac Asimov in the fifties wrote about having to go underground because we have polluted the surface of the earth. These works were twenty and more years ahead of most of us.

PARTICIPANT: *The fantasy and science fiction world gives an opportunity for the exercise of faith in goodness, faith in God, faith in law and order that is harder to believe in than reality.*

ERISMAN: This harks back to the previous question. When you consider someone like J. R. R. Tolkien or C. S. Lewis, who is writing out of a very intense personal commitment, their belief comes through not just in a fantasy world, but in a physical, literal writing of it. That is a comforting thing to hold to you. You can say, 'By golly, this fellow believes in it, why can't I?'

PARTICIPANT: *Do you place literature for minorities — like the blacks and the Native Americans — in a regional setting?*

ERISMAN: The best of it doesn't need to be placed, because it will fit squarely in. I would not place it anywhere. If it is good literature, it will fit right in. And if it is bad, as so much of it is, we should ignore it. I think the worst thing we could do would be to break it out as a separate genre.

NOTES

1. Harry R. Warfel and G. Harrison Orians, 'Introduction,' *American Local-Color Stories* (New York: American Book Co., 1941), p. x.

2. Claude M. Simpson, 'Introduction,' *The Local Colorists: American Short Stories, 1857–1900* (New York: Harper, 1960), pp. 5–7.

3. Warfel and Orians, *American Local-Color Stories*, p. xii.

4. Sarah Orne Jewett, *Betty Leicester* (Boston: Houghton Mifflin, 1889), p. 7.

5. Kate Douglas Wiggin, *A Summer in a Cañon*, *The Writings of Kate Douglas Wiggin* (Boston: Houghton Mifflin, 1917), II, 212. Cited hereafter as *Writings*.

6. Warfel and Orians, *American Local-Color Stories*, p. x.

7. Simpson, *The Local Colorists*, p. 13.

8. Kate Douglas Wiggin, *Rebecca of Sunnybrook Farm*, *Writings*, VI, 105.

9. Warfel and Orians, *American Local-Color Stories*, p. xi.

10. Thomas Bailey Aldrich, *The Story of a Bad Boy*, *The Writings of Thomas Bailey Aldrich* (Boston: Houghton Mifflin, 1911), VII, 152–53.

11. L. Frank Baum, *The Annotated Wizard of Oz*, ed. Michael Patrick Hearn (New York: Clarkson R. Potter, 1973), p. 92.

12. Simpson, *The Local Colorists*, p. 15.

13. Laurence R. Veysey, 'Myth and Reality in Approaching American Regionalism,' *American Quarterly*, 12(1960):31–43.

14. Lewis Mumford, 'Regionalism and Irregionalism,' *Sociological Review*, 20(1928): 18–33; 131–41.

15. Mary Austin, 'Regionalism in American Fiction,' *English Journal*, 21(1932):97–107.

16. Laura Ingalls Wilder, *Little House in the Big Woods* (New York: Harper, 1953), pp. 1–2.

17. Laura Ingalls Wilder, *The Little House on the Prairie* (New York: Harper, 1953), p. 206; Laura Ingalls Wilder, *On the Banks of Plum Creek* (New York: Harper, 1953), pp. 193–208.

18. Marjorie Kinnan Rawlings, *The Yearling* (New York: Scribner, 1939), p. 17.

19. Wilder, *Little House on the Prairie*, p. 247.

20. Rawlings, *The Yearling*, pp. 319–21, 386.

21. Laura Ingalls Wilder, *Farmer Boy* (New York: Harper, 1953), pp. 182–85; *Little House on the Prairie*, pp. 316–17; Laura Ingalls Wilder, *The Long Winter* (New York: Harper, 1953), p. 163.

22. Rawlings, *The Yearling*, pp. 114–20, 405.

23. Blanche Housman Gelfant, *The American City Novel* (Norman: University of Oklahoma, 1954), p. 13.

24. See, for example, Elizabeth Enright, 'The Walnut Shell,' *Doublefields* (London: Heinemann, 1967), pp. 3–18.

25. Elizabeth Enright, *The Saturdays* (New York: Holt, Rinehart, 1941), pp. 14, 28, 54–7, 106.

26. Enright, *The Saturdays*, pp. 141, 31, 20, 99.

27. Yi-Fu Tuan, *Topophilia: A Study of Environmental Perception, Attitudes, and Values* (Englewood Cliffs, New Jersey: Prentice-Hall, 1974), p. 193.

28. Enright, *The Saturdays*, pp. 95–102; Wilder, *The Long Winter*, pp. 288–92, 305–06; Rawlings, *The Yearling*, pp. 197–201.

29. Ralph Waldo Emerson, 'Compensation,' *The Complete Works of Ralph Waldo Emerson*, ed. Edward Waldo Emerson (Boston: Houghton Mifflin, 1903), II, 126–27.

30. Eudora Welty, *Place in Fiction* (New York: House of Books, 1957), pp. 30–1.

31. Daniel J. Boorstin, *The Americans: The Democratic Experience* (New York: Random House, 1973), pp. 166, 246, 557–58.

32. For a recent example, see Natalie Babbitt, 'The Great American Novel for Children—and Why Not,' *Horn Book Magazine*, 50 (1974), 176–85.

33. Veysey, 'Myth and Reality in Approaching American Regionalism,' p. 42.

34. Alvin Toffler, *Future Shock* (New York: Random House, 1970), p. 285.

35. Toffler, *Future Shock*, pp. 336, 335.

36. Welty, *Place in Fiction*, p. 21.

5.

FOREIGN LANGUAGE
PUBLISHING FOR CHILDREN
IN THE UNITED STATES

A Comment on Yiddish, Estonian, Ukrainian, and Armenian Materials

JAMES H. FRASER

Exiled and immigrant peoples who have come to North America in the postcolonial period in many instances recognized their cultural identity for the first time and frequently sought to establish institutions for the preservation of their cultural distinctives considered worthy of retention in the larger society which surrounded them. Joshua Fishman suggests that for most of these immigrating peoples arriving in the late eighteenth and subsequent centuries such group maintenance became a 'conscious goal' only *after* their immigration; but whether the institutions were imported or were a postimmigration development, the fact remains that the fraternal society, the day and religious school, the house of worship, the cultural society, and the press have been the agencies through which the distinctives of the many ethnic groups have been preserved in one form or another through one or more generations. Needless to say, language, a primary factor in preserving ethnic cohesiveness, is that element which precipitates the establishment of the foreign-language press while at the same time being preserved by it. The role of the press in the maintenance of language and other ethnic characteristics is well-known and has been discussed at length by Fishman, Wittke, Haugen, Soltes, Park, and others.[1]

The specific role of children's literature, however, in the language-cultural maintenance process has yet to be scientifically examined for a single language group coming to North America in the post-colonial period. While mention of this type of literature is made by the authors cited above and while extensive discussion of the importance of this literature has appeared in teachers' bulletins and cultural journals of the various language groups, detailed exploration of the question of effectiveness of this sector of publishing in the language-cultural maintenance process or analysis of the content of these printed materials supposedly transmitting elements of the cultural heritage is not known.

In these comments which follow, I am presuming that children's and young people's literature has in its several forms some importance in this process; that the question is worthy of examination; and that if that literature which has been produced in North America with the design to preserve another heritage is to be examined, we must know where it is likely to be found and something of the nature of the institutions which have preserved it.

The standard collection directories, if consulted, would provide with the aid of some imaginative triangulation, a starting place. Lee Ash's *Subject Collections*[2] under the country and language headings will provide a direction to a selection of general language-country collections and institutions where research collections exist. Some contain children's literature and more often than not those in charge of these research institutions will respond to the inquirer specifically seeking children's literature by saying: 'We are a research institution; we do not collect children's literature.' One is not to be deterred by such a response, for often these collections do in fact have such literature or provide through the specialized education and literary journals held by these institutions important leads to individuals and collections.

The national libraries of Canada and the United States have in the past not been the obvious starting places for the researcher looking for holdings of children's and young people's literature produced by the exile or immigrant in transit or the literature produced after arrival. An examination of the children's literature section of *Canadiana* is sufficient to see the place such children's literature has enjoyed. If *Canadiana* accurately reflects that which is held by the National Library of Canada, the collection of French-Canadian juveniles is certainly not comprehensive, to say nothing of Canadian juvenile literature published in Ukrainian, Estonian, Yiddish, Hebrew, German, and other languages. The Library of Congress perhaps can be excused on the grounds that it has a different official purpose, for presumably in the past children's literature in languages other than English has not been necessary in the discharge of its legislative reference responsibility.

State libraries and state historical societies having a responsibility for local imprints have for the most part been unconcerned about the foreign-language children's material produced in communities within the state. There are exceptions such as the Minnesota State Historical Society.

Public libraries in the major cities with a long history of foreign-language publishing have as well all but ignored their role as preservers of locally-produced juvenile books, periodicals, and related materials. Notable exceptions are the Cleveland Public Library, the Research Division of the New York Public Library, and the Central Children's Room of the New York Public Library in recent years. To be sure, scattered items exist in many of the reference collections of the children's rooms in the large public libraries, but a systematic plan to have materials once owned for serving language minorities transferred to the local imprint collection or some other appropriate division is rare indeed. Notorious in their past neglect of the rich local foreign-language publishing heritage for children have been the Chicago and Toledo Public Libraries among others.

College and university libraries awakening to the importance of children's literature in the research process have for the most part come to this awareness too late to have had a part in preserving that which was produced in North America in times past. Many still do not see children's literature within the conspectus of publishing for a given language and thus exclude it categorically. Among the institutions of higher education in which preservation has taken place systematically have been those schools founded by a language minority such as Luther College (Decorah, Iowa), Suomi College (Hancock, Michigan), Gustavus Adolphus College (St. Peter, Minnesota), Bethel College (North Newton, Kansas).

The collections which we are seeking are to be found, in addition to those which we have mentioned above, in the libraries of day and religious schools, sectarian theological schools, fraternal and cultural organizations, churches and synagogues, ethnic publishing houses, and research institutions dedicated in some way to the preservation of specific language-cultural elements.

These collections defy generalization as to organization of materials, conditions under which they are maintained, or acquisition policy. Classification may range from a meticulously maintained card catalog to a helter-skelter shelf arrangement that is subject oriented at best. The condition of materials themselves may be one of sad deterioration from overuse and being housed in rooms with extreme temperatures, or the items may be well preserved and properly housed, although the latter is rare and usually applies to but a small portion of the juvenile titles in a given collection. The attitude toward acquisition ranges from condescending to warm appreciation of the importance of these materials.

The origin of the materials existing in these collections and broadly classed as juvenile literature, e.g., textbooks, recreational reading, and periodicals can, however, be neatly categorized into (1) those materials published in the mother country or countries in the case of a dispersed language, e.g., Yiddish or Ukrainian, (2) those materials published in transit, that is, published in the process of migration from one region to another, e.g., Ukrainian, Estonian, Polish, and (3) those materials published in the country of destination, e.g., the United States or Canada.

My present purpose is to elaborate on the types of collections which exist and in which material may be found. Examples from the experience of Yiddish, Estonian, Ukrainian, and Armenian language groups have been chosen to illustrate specific approaches in the production and preservation of materials.

These language groups also reflect specific histories of language maintenance and existence in North America. Yiddish, a language in which publishing for children flourished for nearly thirty years in the United States for the benefit of a first generation born here, declined markedly and was in a sense rediscovered by a third generation in the late 1960s and 1970s with a moderate increase in publishing. While Estonian speakers have been in North America for several generations, only the post–World War II migration produced a literature other than a popular press and with the second generation has experienced a decline. Ukrainian, which again has a history of periodical and newspaper publishing for two generations in North America, produced a literature for children primarily in the post–World War II period. Ukrainian publishing, centered mainly in Toronto and the New York City area, is being maintained with effort despite the pressures toward acculturation. Armenian acculturation for two generations has been the rule rather than the exception and at no time has there been a significant language-maintenance program with accompanying literature for children or young people until the past three years. At the moment, however, an effective experiment in Armenian publishing and language maintenance is taking place through the foresight of the president of the Armenian General Benevolent Union, who has retained two individuals to produce an impressive array of texts, games, and collateral reading materials.

Now to the collections.

More has been written on Yiddish children's and youth literature in North America than any other, exclusive of English language children's literature. The newsletters of the education division of the Workmen's Circle, the Sholem Aleichem Folk Institute, the Service Bureau for Jewish Education (an outgrowth of the Jewish Peoples Fraternal Order), and the Board of Jewish Education (formerly the Jewish Education Committee) have in aggregate numerous references and articles on the importance of this literature in book, periodical, and textbook form. The majority of these articles are in Yiddish.

The numerical extent of the books themselves which have survived has been indicated by Fraser in 1972.[3] More recently Abramowicz has given us an historical sketch of this literature.[4] For an indication of the productivity in North America from 1911 to 1946 one can refer to Kazdan,[5] who cites two hundred forty titles published in that thirty-five-year period. Textbooks and songbooks for youth, however, appeared as early as the 1890s but were few in number. The post–World War II period saw a decline in Yiddish literature for children with brief revivals of interest in the mid-1950s and then again in the 1960s and 1970s. These cycles of interest have necessitated the reprinting of earlier works as well as re-editing others and in some cases publishing new titles. It is interesting to note that the first English-Yiddish/Yiddish-English dictionary for children and youth was not published in the flourishing period of the 1920s or 1930s but rather in 1968.[6]

In all the publishing for children in Yiddish, the quantity has been based on the demand for literature within the various Yiddish school systems which now in total population number somewhere between forty-five hundred and five thousand in the United States and Canada.

The Yivo Institute for Jewish Research in New York City has two components in its history. An institute and library were created in Vilna following a planning meeting of Jewish scholars in Berlin in 1925. This library was taken by the invading German army in 1941 and hidden in Germany. It was found in the American Zone of Occupation at the close of the war and brought to New York where it joined the library of the American Branch of Yivo.[7]

The more than three thousand children's books, periodicals, and other pieces of juvenile ephemera in the library are not segregated but are accessible through the classed headings in the card catalog. Originally this collection contained mainly juvenile Yiddica published in Central Europe. Now juvenile Yiddica from all over the world including the United States is systematically acquired. There are no exclusions by form, age group, or place of imprint. The librarian of Yivo, Dina Abramowicz, is also the compiler of an annual bibliography of Yiddica, including children's books, which appears in the *Jewish Book Annual*.

The Bund Archives of the Jewish Labor Movement is a collection which has moved from country to country like that of the Yivo library and which contains considerable children's material although only a few items from North America. This archive was formed in Geneva seventy-seven years ago as a means for preserving those books, pamphlets, periodicals, and posters which had little chance of surviving in any archive of Eastern Europe except that of the tsarist Ochrana. As a resource for the clandestine publications of this movement prior to the October Revolution, there is no collection its equal. The odyssey of this collection from Geneva to Berlin during World War I, to Paris in 1933, its abandonment by the Nazis in an open field at the end of the occupation, its recovery and final trip to New York City, is as exciting as the story of the Yivo library.

The materials of interest to us are the Bund's periodicals published for children and young people and approximately one thousand volumes including pamphlets printed in Poland and Lithuania for the use of Yiddish language schools having a partisan orientation.

Like Yivo, the material is cataloged and available to the serious scholar. One problem existing in both collections is the fragility of much of the material. The majority of the newspapers and periodicals are in need of immediate attention. Many issues of some titles have already disintegrated to the point where there is textual loss. It is an unfortunate commentary on our time that materials with the wartime adventures which these have experienced should disintegrate now on the Upper East Side of Manhattan only for lack of money.

The Library of the Board of Jewish Education in New York is primarily a reference library for the staff of the Board and researchers in the field of traditional and religious Jewish education. The children's literature held by the library consists mainly of Hebrew and Yiddish readers, primers, and collateral reading materials. The total number of titles in Hebrew is more than six hundred while that in Yiddish is slightly over one hundred. The collection is not cataloged but is arranged on shelves alphabetically by author within the two language groups. Acquisition of material in the past was based on the need of the library, and was, therefore, not comprehensive. The collection has not been developed to any degree in the past three years because of space and financial limitations. However, the collection is still available for research. Although the collection is small it deserves mention here for the content of the works, whether published in the United States or elsewhere, tends to have a traditionalist and religious viewpoint.

The Jewish Theological Seminary Library of New York contains a small sample of religious Yiddica for children and young people. Currently the library collects children's books in Yiddish and English by Yiddish writers who write for both adults and children. The acquisition of children's books and periodicals is highly selective and is determined on merit and potential usefulness at the time the collection is offered to the library as a gift or for sale. No limitations by place or period-of-imprint are made.

The Jewish Division of the New York Public Library has to some degree assumed a 'local history' responsibility for acquiring Yiddish and Hebrew children's literature from the New York City area as well as from other parts of the world.

Many rare and scarce titles are in this collection, including nearly forty runs of Yiddish and Hebrew children's and youth periodicals from New York City, Vienna, Tel Aviv, Warsaw, Vilna, Riga, Lugansk, and elsewhere. With but few exceptions, the periodicals were published in the twentieth century with the majority of runs beginning in the 1920s.

The Jewish Division does not exclude materials by form or subject matter. A broadside, poster, periodical, or book is acquired when considered of importance to the collection. In the last two or three years, however, there has not been quite the acquisitions enthusiasm in this area as formerly.

A number of titles in this collection are not cataloged but are found together with other pamphlet-form materials. A collective heading in the catalog directs the user to such materials.

In an inventory taken by the author in 1970 of juvenile Yiddica held in a number of North American libraries for the decades from 1890 through the 1960s, the Jewish Division of the New York Public Library had a total of ninety-three titles in comparison with eighty-eight titles held by the Library of the Board of Jewish Education in New York City and some sixty-seven titles held by the Hebraic Section of the Library of Congress. Approximately two hundred seventy titles were published in North America during the period covered by the inventory.[8]

The libraries of the organizations which have published the greatest quantity of juvenile Yiddica in the United States contain an important resource, for they contain not only most of their own titles but frequently titles from other publishers as well. In New York City the libraries of the Workmen's Circle, the Service Bureau for Jewish Education, and the Sholem Aleichem Folk Institute represent the largest collections in this category. These collections are maintained primarily for the teachers in the school system and those editors preparing material to be used by the teachers and children.

In the case of the Workmen's Circle Education Department with more than twenty-one hundred children and young people in its schools in the United States and Canada, there is a continuing need for materials. Twenty-two titles excluding workbooks and songbooks are included in their current list of in-print books.

These and earlier titles are all on the shelves in a reference collection that numbers some one hundred seventy-five titles for children and young people. It should also be mentioned that the Workmen's Circle has published a children's periodical, *Kinderzeitung*, since the early 1920s. A complete file is available in the editorial library.

Juvenile Yiddica published in this country as well as throughout the world is available for research purposes and is in substantial quantity.

Peoples from the Baltic countries who have come to the United States and Canada, particularly in the post–World War II period, have established a few publishing agencies. In transit, Estonian, Lithuanian, and Latvian scouting groups established printing activities in the displaced-persons camps of Western Europe. Scouting periodicals (usually mimeographed), songbooks, and guides were the principal types of material produced. When dispersed to Sweden, Australia, Canada, Latin America, South Africa, and the United States, these groups continued to publish for children and young people small amounts of the materials mentioned as well as primers and readers, books of poetry, anthologies of national literature, and compendia of nonfiction written during the period of migration.

The titles in print at the time of this writing are few in number and consist of a series of textbooks published recently in Sweden and miscellaneous titles published in the 1960s and early 1970s in Canada, Sweden, and the United States. Publishing for such a small number of individuals has never been economically feasible and has, therefore, been subsidized privately or by the government in the case of text materials published in Sweden and Canada. The textbooks which have been recently produced in Sweden and Canada are in editions of one thousand to fifteen hundred.

The Estonian children's literature in the United States has been the work of three or four single-minded individuals. The most notable has been Meemi Malgi, formerly a teacher and stringed instrument maker. In the United States Malgi has relied upon his skill as violin and Kannel maker (the Kannel is the Estonian national instrument) to provide an income. Malgi founded the Eesti Koolitoimkond (Estonian School Committee), a one-man committee, and arranged with six Estonian authors to write nine books for children with the express purpose of providing uplifting material for the eleven to fifteen year old. The books were published in editions of one thousand titles or less. Some of the titles were more successful than others and all were published in the 1960s. Scouting materials, together with a children's page once a month in the two Estonian papers of Toronto and 'Vaba Eesti Soña' in New York City, constitute the sole additional literature in Estonian in North America at this time. These materials are available in the publishing offices of the newspapers serving the Estonian community as well as in the day and Saturday school offices. (There are seventy weekend schools in the greater New York area and two hundred in the Toronto area with a total of fifteen hundred students for all of North America.)[10]

Of the fifty-three Estonian titles for children published in North America in the period 1944–1970,[11] it is interesting to note that the Library of Congress holds one and the National Library of Canada none, according to the annual volumes of *Canadiana.*

Ukrainian children's literature in North America has, like Estonian, been primarily a post–World War II activity. While the first North American Ukrainian children's title was a primer published in Winnipeg in 1904, the pre–World War I and between-the-wars migrations did not bring the number of writers fleeing the Ukraine as did the post–World War II migration.

Ukrainian children's literature in this period of migration has been largely imaginative literature. Textbooks, of course, have been produced, but works of poetry, stories, fiction, and biography far outnumber them. No bibliography of North American Juvenile Ukrainica exists. Yet, like Estonian literature and Latvian literature published outside of the country of origin, one can, if patient, identify much through bibliographies which have been published by various national institutes.

Research and national libraries have again ignored the children's book and research in their acquisitions, and in the case of Ukrainica this is surprising, for the volume has been larger and the visibility of the Ukrainian on the American scene has been greater perhaps than that of any other national group from Central Europe.

The researcher into this literature is again dependent upon publisher's archives, the day and religious school library, and the institution serving the specific needs of this language minority.

The Ukrainian National Library and Museum in Chicago reportedly has a substantial amount of the nearly one hundred fifty titles (this does not include the reprints of Howerla) published in North America since the early 1950s. The Ukrainian Academy of Arts and Sciences in New York City also collects children's books assiduously from North America as well as those produced in other Ukrainian communities around the world exclusive of the USSR.

The Slavonic Division of the New York Public Library Research Division has a modest collection and is one of the few general public libraries to take an interest in this area. The central children's room of the New York Public Library has as well a sampling of that Ukrainica published in New York City. The reference collections of children's books in the branches, notably the Thompkins Square branch, also have some examples.

Ukrainian children's literature published in North America is not as easy to acquire as one might initially think, despite the organization of children's authors and illustrators into an association which gives its stamp of approval to those works which meet its standards. The author-illustrator team commonly enters into an agreement with a printer willing to take the risk. The books are then distributed by the bookshops, cultural associations, as well as by the printer himself. The principal means of announcement is the Ukrainian press and word of mouth.

There are, however, established publishers of newspapers who have engaged in publishing books for children as well. *Svoboda*, in Jersey City, has published a Ukrainian daily since 1897. In 1954 it began publishing a children's periodical, *Veselka*, under the editorship of Walter Barahura. The periodical was in one sense an outgrowth of a children's page in *Svoboda* which had appeared sporadically through the years. This periodical began with a circulation of some five thousand and has maintained itself at that level during the school year, declining to thirty-five hundred during the summer. Seventy-five percent of this circulation has been within North America. With this audience, *Svoboda*, which is an organ of the Ukrainian National Association, undertook to publish children's books as well and between 1955 and 1966 published five titles with editions of two to three thousand. But it took nearly two years to sell out an edition, and it has since discontinued publishing except for the periodical.

The majority of children's and young people's titles are now published in Canada, where there is a much larger market. A few continue to be published in this country, however, by such organizations as the Ukrainian National Woman's Association of New York and some inexpensive reprints of older Ukrainian titles by Howerla of New York City. All in all, there are no more than six publishers currently publishing Ukrainian children's books; the rest remain private undertakings as described above.

Ukrainian children's literature, like Yiddish, is of a substantial quantity and provides a varied resource for the scholar. Like Yiddish, one cannot generalize on the content, for religious and partisan factors exist here as well.[12]

Until 1972, Armenian children's literature in America was insignificant in quantity. There was some form of occasional religious papers produced in diocesan offices and mimeographed teacher's materials for the religious schools charged with the responsibility of maintaining the language along with religious instruction. The material was supplemented with textbooks and some recreational reading printed in Beirut. (Because of a distinct difference in the Western and Eastern Armenian languages, Armenian children's literature produced in the Armenian SSR could not be used.)

In 1972 with a total enrollment in the day and weekend schools of around fifteen hundred, the situation was not encouraging. In that year two individuals appeared on the scene, and if their initial success at reviving interest in a language through the use of imaginative texts (which they have created as well as teaching materials and collateral readers) is a portent of the future, we may see a literature for children develop that in style may serve as a model for other ethnic minorities desiring language and cultural revitalization.

Today approximately six thousand Armenian children and

young people are in day and weekend schools, kindergarten to high school, throughout North America. Immigration of recent years during the unrest in the Middle East has accounted for only a modest part of this increase. Not all of these children can read fluently. In fact, it is estimated that only two thousand can read well; yet the trend is definitely upward.[13]

The plans for a literature program being developed now by the Armenian Language Laboratory under the direction of Silva der Stephanian include additions to the seven already-produced integrated textbooks with accompanying teachers' manuals, tapes, and transparencies. Included as well is a series of fifty collateral reading works of imaginative literature. Games and puzzles have also been produced and a children's periodical is in the planning stage.

These books are available in the Diocesan Archives, the day schools and the Mekhitarist Library in Boston as well as the Mekhitarist Library in Rome (the largest repository of Armenian literature outside the Armenian National Library in Erevan).

To conclude this rambling commentary, it is clear from the data presented that resources are available for the study of the children's and young people's literature of the American ethnic minorities discussed. However, this literature is not available where one would normally expect to find it, e.g. the large general research collection. Instead, the researcher must make use of the collections in the institutions developed by the various language minorities.

NOTES

1. Joshua A. Fishman, et al., *Language Loyalty in the United States* (The Hague: Mouton, 1966), p. 27.
   Carl Wittke, *The German Language Press in America* (Lexington: University of Kentucky Press, 1957).
   Einar I. Haugen, *The Norwegian Language in America*, 2 vols. (Philadelphia: University of Pennsylvania Press, 1953).
   Mordecai Soltes, *The Yiddish Press: An Americanizing Agency* (New York: Teachers College, Columbia University, 1923).
   Robert Ezra Park, *The Immigrant Press and Its Control* (New York: Harper, 1922).

2. Lee Ash, *Subject Collections*, 4th ed. (New York: Bowker, 1974).

3. James H. Fraser, 'Foreign Language Children's Literature in the United States' (New York: Columbia University, Dissertation, 1972).

4. Dina Abramowicz, 'Yiddish Juvenilia: Ethnic Survival in the New World,' *Wilson Library Bulletin*, 50(October 1975):138–45.

5. Hayyim Kazdan, 'Finf-un-draysik Yor Yidishe Kinder Literatur,' *Shulpinkes* (Chicago: Sholem Aleichem Folk Institute, 1946), pp. 335–79.

6. Aaron Bergman, *Student's Dictionary, English-Yiddish, Yiddish-English; A Popular Dictionary for School and Home*, Itche Goldberg, ed. (New York: Kinderbuch Publishers, 1968).

7. Dina Abramowicz, 'Yivo Library,' *Jewish Book Annual* 25(1967–68):89–90.

8. Kazdan, *op. cit.*, and volumes of the *Jewish Book Annual* have provided the basis for this estimate.

9. Interview with Liivi Lepik, May 3, 1976.

10. Ibid.

11. Bernard Kangro, *Eesti Raamat Vabas Maailmas* (Lund, Sweden: Eesti Kirjanike Kooperatiiv, 1971).

12. Interview with Walter Barahura, April 2, 1976.

13. Interview with Silva der Stephanian, April 21, 1976.

6.
IN FOR A PENNY,
IN FOR A POUND

Or, Some Economic Aspects
Of Collecting Eighteenth- and Early
Nineteenth-Century Books for Children,
With Reflections on the Sources of
Such Books, the Prices Now Paid for
Them, and the Best Remedy for the
Pain Those Prices Give the Purchaser,
All Simply Stated by a Long-Sufferer

HOWELL HEANEY

Our program suggests that I should direct my remarks to the economic aspects of the collecting of eighteenth-century books for children. In accepting that charge my situation is, in some respects, like that of a man called on to discuss the prospects of saving the Indian and his way of life just after the Battle of the Little Big Horn—not hopeless, but certainly difficult. Since what may be said of collecting children's books of the eighteenth century is rapidly becoming true of those published before 1821, you will, I hope, allow me to enlarge the scope of my survey to include the first twenty years of the nineteenth century, rounding it out to the period covered by d'Alté A. Welch's *Bibliography of American Children's Books Printed Prior to 1821* (Worcester and Barre, American Antiquarian Society and Barre Publishers, 1972). Since my experience in collecting books for children for the past twenty years has been in helping to enlarge the Rosenbach Collection of Early American Children's Books at the Free Library of Philadelphia, you will understand my drawing examples from that experience.

Let us consider the growth of the Rosenbach Collection as typical of the growth of similar collections, and then move on to a consideration of the availability of eighteenth- and early nineteenth-century books for children today, the trend in prices asked for them over the past thirty-five years, and the situation in which, as collectors, we now find ourselves.

The Rosenbach Collection had its beginnings about 1835 when Dr. Rosenbach's uncle, Moses Polock, then a clerk of eighteen with M'Carty and Davis of Philadelphia, began collecting the books for children published by them, and by their predecessors Johnson and Warner and Jacob Johnson. A collector first and a very reluctant seller of books second, Moses Polock built on the nucleus of his earliest purchases for more than sixty years. In 1900 he gave the collection to the Doctor, who, with his sisters, added to it substantially over the next forty-seven years. In period the collection was limited to books published before 1837. In scope it included books for children printed in what is now the

United States, wherever written, with the emphasis on books which the young might have enjoyed, although this emphasis was modified by the stern nature of the earlier material.

As a collector of books for children Dr. Rosenbach was in an enviable position, for great masses of books passed through his hands, he was in touch with sellers, scouts, and fellow dealers throughout this country and abroad, and the majority of the books he wanted for this collection were little valued or sought after. To cite an example illustrating that last point, Ernest J. Wessen of the Midland Rare Book Company of Mansfield, Ohio, told me of visiting the Doctor in the depths of the Depression hoping to sell him a lot of manuscripts. The Doctor's depression was as deep as that of the country, and he was not buying. Wessen was so moved by Rosenbach's state that, to cheer him up, he gave him a copy of *Punctuation Personified* (Steubenville, Ohio, 1831), a delightful book based on an English original, with sprightly hand-colored engravings by Hugh Anderson. Wessen said had he known how scarce the book was he would never have made the gift. To such gifts were added regular purchases and exchanges, notably with the American Antiquarian Society.

In 1947 Dr. Rosenbach presented his collection, then numbering more than eight hundred fifty books, to the Free Library of Philadelphia, and in the thirty years since—and especially in the years following Ellen Shaffer's appointment as Rare Book Librarian of the Free Library in 1954—the collection has increased sevenfold, through purchases and gifts. The largest of our additions by gift have come from the American Sunday-School Union and from Mr. and Mrs. Emerson Greenaway. In 1962 the Sunday-School Union presented the Free Library with a nearly complete run of its publications from 1824 to 1900, together with publications of its predecessor, the Sunday and Adult School Union, dating from 1817 to 1824. The ground from which this gift sprang was broken in the late 1940s when Franklin Price, then Librarian of the Free Library, approached the officers of the Sunday-School Union with the suggestion that such a gift would be to the advantage of both institutions, and the possibility of the gift was carefully cultivated between 1951 and 1962 by Emerson Greenaway, Mr. Price's successor, and by Ellen Shaffer.

The books published before 1837 in this collection number nearly two thousand. In 1971 Mr. and Mrs. Greenaway gave the Library their collection of books for children, over a thousand volumes published in this country between 1765 and 1900, two hundred and fifty-five of them within the Rosenbach period.

This brief account of the Rosenbach Collection illustrates the various ways in which a collection can grow. Whatever our situation in the future may be, our growth will be governed by the nature of the collection and what its use is perceived to be, the availability of desirable books, and the prices asked for those books measured against the funds we have to spend. I should say here that our purchases are made entirely from gifts and the income from trust funds, especially a fund provided for in the will of Simon Gratz.

An understanding of the nature of the collection one intends to build is basic to all other decisions. Dr. Rosenbach's, as I have suggested, emphasized the books that children read by choice, although for the seventeenth and much of the eighteenth century that choice was limited. *The Rule of the New Creature* (Boston, 1682), the earliest work in the collection, begins: 'Be sensible of thy Original Corruption daily how it inclines thee to evil . . .' and the tone of most of the books of the next hundred years hews close to that line. As late as 1831 the moral is driven home, for in *Punctuation Personified* the verses on the period run:

> This full fac'd gentleman here shewn,
> To all my friends, no doubt, is known:
> In him the PERIOD we behold,
> Who stands his ground whilst four are told;
> And always ends a perfect sentence,
> As 'Crime is follow'd by Repentance.'

Our modification of Dr. Rosenbach's purpose has been in the direction of adding influential textbooks of the late eighteenth and early nineteenth century in their earliest, and earliest Philadelphia editions, and representative examples of books on child care and education, but our emphasis is on adding the sort of books that form the major portion of the collection, those which are to be found in Welch or would qualify for admission there. We have also expanded the range of the collection to include examples of early books for children from as far away as Hawaii, and, on occasion, its range in date, for example, to include early books for children printed in Alaska.

Let us now consider the availability of eighteenth- and early nineteenth-century American children's books today. I approached the writing of this paper with the notion that the supply of such books was rapidly diminishing under the pressure of growing demand, and so it is. When Dr. Rosenbach published the catalog of his collection[1] in 1933, it included two hundred sixty works printed in the eighteenth century. Our purchases between 1955 and 1976 have added three hundred ninety eighteenth-century books to the collection, half as many again as came to us in 1947 from Dr. Rosenbach. The Greenaway gift of 1971 added another twenty-four. As a final bench mark, sixty books published in the eighteenth century were offered in the Swann Sale of February 1976[2] but all of them belonged to the latter part of the century and most of them were texts or guides to morals and manners. The comparable figures for books published in the years from 1801 through 1820 are three hundred thirty-four in the Rosenbach catalog of 1933, 1,154 added by purchase between 1955 and 1976, eighty-seven in the Greenaway gift, and two hundred and forty offered in the Swann Sale.

It does not appear from these figures that any of us need despair of continuing to add significant works published in the early nineteenth century to our collection, but we are well past the period, for books of the eighteenth century, where supply and demand were in relative equilibrium. We are, however, better served in acquiring nineteenth-century books for children than Moses Polock ever was, and perhaps better served than Dr. Rosenbach was. Until recently the number of collectors of early books for children was relatively small, and the sources on which they could draw limited.

A lively interest in the New England Primer can be traced as far back as George Livermore's articles in *The Cambridge Chronicle*, gathered in *The Origin, History and Character of the New England*

Primer published by the author in an edition of twelve copies in 1849. This pioneer work was reprinted by Charles F. Heartman in New York in 1915, and followed by Heartman's bibliography *The New England Primer Issued Prior to* 1830. The first edition of that bibliography appeared in 1914, the second in 1922, and the third in 1934. Other special studies were published over the years, but it was not until the appearance of the catalog of the Rosenbach Collection in 1933 that the collector, as distinguished from the student, had a general guide to the field of early American books for children.

During the same period books for children, beginning with the New England Primer, were offered in booksellers' and auction catalogs, but it is only recently that there have been catalogs devoted entirely to such books. The year 1941 saw the appearance of two major catalogs, Walter Schatzki's *Old and Rare Children's Books* (New York: 1941; reprinted at Detroit by the Gale Research Co. in 1974) in which forty-four of the two hundred sixteen lots were American, and Edward Morrill & Son's *American Children's Books, 1723–1939. Catalogue Six* (Boston: 1941) in which 1,187 lots were listed. The appearance of booksellers who specialize in children's literature is a development of the last fifteen years, and in the same period there have been catalogs of children's books from numerous dealers whose business is of a more general nature. In February of 1967 Sotheby's held the first of its regular series of auctions of children's books and juvenilia in London, presently scheduled quarterly, and this February the Swann Galleries held an auction of children's books in New York. These efforts are supported by a growing group of collectors, and may be related to the publication of d'Alté Welch's bibliography cited above, which appeared in installments in the *Proceedings* of the American Antiquarian Society from April of 1963 through October of 1967 and then in revised form, as a bound volume, in 1972. With the publication of this great work, all concerned with earlier books for children published in what is now the United States acquired a reliable, if not infallible, guide to the importance and relative rarity of the books they were buying, selling, and collecting—and that expensive, and sometimes misapplied, phrase, 'Not in Welch.'

The word 'expensive' suggests the next subject we should consider, the price of early books for children. The heart of this matter was neatly summed up over a hundred years ago by that great bookseller, auctioneer, and bibliographer Joseph Sabin: 'If a book is unique and nobody wants it, it is worthless. If a book is unique and two people want it, it is worth the bottom dollar of the richer of the two.'

It takes neither wide experience nor deep research to establish the fact that the trend of prices of books for children over the past thirty-five years has been sharply upward. A comparison of the prices asked for a sampling of eighteenth- and early nineteenth-century books for children in Morrill's catalog of 1941, a Morrill catalog of 1963 (*Children's Books, Catalogue* 102), and in dealers' catalogs over the past twenty years, with those realized for the same books at the Swann sale of February 1976 is interesting. In making the comparisons at least the dealers' commission of 10 percent should be added to the prices paid at the Swann auction.

John Aikin's *Letters from a Father to His Son* (Philadelphia: 1796) was offered by Morrill in 1963 for $7.50 and brought $14.00 at the Swann sale. John Gregory's *A Father's Legacy* (Philadelphia: 1787) was offered in 1963 at $13.50 and brought $25.00 at the Swann sale. Nicholas Pike's *New and Complete System of Arithmetic* in its first edition (Newbury-Port: 1788) was offered by Morrill in 1941 at $7.50 and brought $30.00 at the Swann sale.

Moving to the period 1801 to 1820, Arnaud Berquin's *The Beauties of The Children's Friend* (Boston: 1808) was offered by Morrill in 1941 at $6.00 and brought $25.00 at the Swann sale. *Gay's Fables* (Philadelphia: 1808) was offered by Morrill in 1941 at $5.00 and again in 1963 at $12.50, and realized $30.00 at the Swann sale. *The Young Child's ABC* (New York: 1820) was offered by Morrill in 1941 at $2.50 and brought $30.00 at the Swann sale. In the case of titles in Welch, prices at the Swann sale were generally two to three times those at which the same titles were offered in the late 1950s and the early 1960s.

Any conclusions to be drawn from these comparisons should take into account the following additional facts. While the prices realized by eighteenth-century non-Welch titles at the Swann sale were generally below the estimates of knowledgeable authorities, prices for considerable rarities listed in Welch were within or slightly above those estimates, for example *The Holy Bible Abridged* (New York: 1790) with a woodcut by the nine-year-old Peter Maverick (Lot 119), which brought $220.00, *Mrs. Pleasant's Story Book* (Philadelphia: 1798), hitherto known only from an advertisement (Lot 683), which brought $325.00, and *Tommy Thoroughgood* (Stonington: 1800) of which only one copy is located by Welch (Lot 929), which brought $190.00. Prices for books published from 1801 through 1820 were often below and sometimes well below the estimates, especially in the case of non-Welch items, but this may be accounted for in part by the very considerable number of items offered at once.

Let me close with a few thoughts on the situation in which libraries now find themselves. We can no more expect to keep prices from rising by our own action than King Canute expected to stop the rising of the tide by his command. Although libraries are major purchasers of early children's books, they are by no means the only purchasers. While our withdrawing from the market would certainly affect prices in some degree, the competition amongst private collectors would continue. In periods or instances in which we are convinced that prices are too high we ought to lie low. Sir Thomas Phillipps justified the prices he paid for manuscripts on the ground that the value he set on those he purchased resulted in saving manuscripts generally. Certainly the value of early books for children has been established, and they are as secure from destruction as price can make them. Sir Thomas's excuse will no longer serve us.

In passing up a possible purchase an institution has an advantage over the private collector, for there is a greater possibility of its having a second chance to buy the same title. An institution may even hope that the book it wanted will eventually be given to it, for the tax laws still favor institutions as recipients of gifts of books. If the generosity of donors extends, as Dr. Rosenbach's did, to allowing the sale of duplicates, gifts will make the improvement of copies and even further expansion of the collection possible.

The experience of libraries proves the importance that gifts have in the growth of collections, but the acceptance of a major gift implies not only a willingness to organize and make available the material received, but also to expand the collection through further acquisitions. The scope of that expansion depends on the availability of funds. Its success will depend on the help of the booksellers, and at an auction on the help of a single bookseller, who ought to be a man with both feet on the ground and usually one ear, too.

In buying, competition for rarities for the sake of making an impression should certainly be avoided, for it only drives up prices needlessly. A book at the American Antiquarian Society or the Library of Congress is part of the common wealth, and I am glad to say that all of those in the Rosenbach Collection which would bear filming are now available on microfiche. While this form of reproduction will not serve all users, it will serve most, and helps to preserve the originals as well.

It has been suggested that the funds of each of us might be made to go further if our areas of responsibility were more clearly defined. Surely we already have the means at hand to avoid needless duplication. For most of us, limited funds will reinforce common sense. The surest guarantee of sound action in spending those funds lies in a wide knowledge of our own collections and those of others, in an ever-widening knowledge of the books offered us, and in a spirit of cooperation amongst all of those interested in the growth of collections of books for children — dealers, collectors, librarians, and scholars.

NOTES

1. Abraham Simon Wolf Rosenbach, *Early American Children's Books* (Portland, Maine: The Southworth Press, 1933; reprinted: New York: Kraus Reprint Corporation, 1966; New York: Dover Publications, Inc., 1971).

2. Swann Galleries, Inc., New York, *Children's Books, Including the Collection of the Late Benjamin Tighe. Public Auction Sale Number 1015. Thursday, February 26– Friday, February 27* (New York: Swann Galleries, Inc., 1976). A very considerable portion of the books offered came from the collection of Edgar S. Oppenheimer, and in all some forty consignors contributed to the sale.

7.
RANDOM NOTES ON THE PRESERVATION OF EIGHTEENTH- AND NINETEENTH-CENTURY CHILDREN'S BOOKS

FREDERICK E. BAUER, JR.

Justification for a commitment of time and treasure to the preservation of eighteenth- and nineteenth-century children's books need not be debated before this assembly of librarians and literary scholars. But, unless we librarians and literary scholars are forceful and convincing to those who create and administer budgets, unless we argue with conviction that there is an emergency in our collections, there will be very little left of the rich heritage of early American children's books when the American Tricentennial is celebrated.

Although justification need not be made for remarks about preservation of early American children's books, an explanation of the basis for the remarks is in order.

Preservation is an action term that suggests a variety of measures which are needed to protect text and artifact.

You will note that I include only eighteenth- and nineteenth-century children's books in this discussion. However, I am not prepared to argue that these are more or less important than similar English imprints, or foreign language imprints, or children's books of the twentieth century. I know that the ones of which I speak are important, and I know that you share this view.

Recently I went browsing through the modest study done by Harry Weiss in 1939 entitled *Little Red Riding Hood: A Terror Tale of the Nursery*. Now, it must be admitted that this tale has been around a long time and has been read by millions of us as children; but, it is seldom considered as something worthy of special attention. In his study, Mr. Weiss appended a check list which identified fifty-nine bibliographically important editions of this common Perrault folktale. The list included sixteen American imprints of which one-half were eighteenth- and nineteenth-century editions. And, of these eight, most were scarce, many were rare, and at least one was unique and is now held by the Free Library of Philadelphia.

The distinguished catalogs of the Osborne Collection which were so carefully prepared by Judith St. John contain at least twenty-eight entries of French and British editions which contain the *Little Red Riding Hood* story. Most of the volumes cited are scarce, many of them are rare, and a number of them are unique.

In the collections of the American Antiquarian Society, I have counted thirty-two American editions of the *Little Red Riding Hood* tale. Eleven of these imprints are included in the d'Alté Welch bibliography, and twenty-one of them are from the period 1840 to 1870. Among these latter mid-nineteenth-century editions, there are ten *different* versions of the tale. And some of these books are scarce, a few are rare, and almost all of them are discolored, or stained, or brittle, or mutilated. They are, after all, well-used children's books.

This examination of the works in our collection revealed to me that the traditional folk story which was first written down by Charles Perrault in the latter years of the seventeenth century underwent considerable change in the eighteenth and again the nineteenth century and has become a somewhat different story in our own time. In at least one article written by Eric Fromm, the story is retold in a much different fashion. It is not the same folktale which is used as a 'Freudian' illustration of the 'classic' male-female struggle in the conflict between Little Red Riding Hood and the wolf.

The article by Lee Burns in *Children's Literature* for 1969 does not recount the folktale as it appears in the original, but instead reflects the variations of time.

My reason for introducing these observations about extant copies of *Little Red Riding Hood* is simply to underline my basic assumption that eighteenth- and nineteenth-century children's books are cultural artifacts as well as purveyors of social and literary history. And, I am convinced that they are in critically short supply and now suffer from indifference. My obvious conclusion is that these volumes must be preserved for the scholars of today and for the students of tomorrow who care about the circumstances of life as well as the artifacts of yesterday.

To identify some areas of the vast field of preservation, these comments will be limited to topics and conditions which have been identified in questioning other librarians. Each of the four aspects selected will be dealt with very quickly with the hope that further investigation and study will be possible when the excitement of this seminar becomes corroded by routine. These random notes will touch upon the priorities, the process, the problems and the promise of preservation.

PRIORITIES

The primary step which must be taken by all of us if we really intend to preserve early American children's books is to decide exactly what needs to be done first, second, and third. Not everyone will come up with the same list in the same order. Priorities, after all, have a strong individual and institutional cast to them. In some cases the objectives of the researcher may differ markedly from those of the librarian. But, no one can argue that the overriding goal is to preserve these materials so that there will always be access to the rich variety of information which is revealed by the children's literature of earlier times. If providing access is the agreed-upon objective, then we must decide upon the proper steps to move in that direction.

The most immediate step needed is to stabilize the storage and handling conditions. This step is preventive maintenance and includes procedures which are more or less within the control of the librarian. Cleanliness of stacks; use of neutral paper, envelopes, and boxes; stability of temperature and humidity; protection from fire, theft, and vandalism. These are the kinds of conditions which will retard decay and buy time for the planning and executing of more elaborate and specialized preservation measures.

The second order of business is to microfilm the best available copy of each extant edition of each children's book to preserve the text.

Although I am speaking now of eighteenth- and nineteenth-century children's books, the fact is that we also ought to be concerned about late nineteenth- and early twentieth-century books as well. Unhappily, these latter works are going to suffer from more rapid deterioration than their earlier counterparts.

Efficiency and economy demand that a microfilming effort be cooperative and nationwide and based upon a sound bibliography. There are a number of current projects which can serve as models or as a nucleus—projects done by Kraus-Thomson, Ltd., and the Readex Microprint Corporation. Unfortunately, however, the bibliography of children's books after 1820 is incomplete if even extant. And, at the moment, there is no ground swell of demand among libraries to purchase yet another collection in microform. Nevertheless and despite these difficulties, I suggest that our second priority should be a plan for insuring the microform publication of all extant editions of children's books published in America in the eighteenth and nineteenth centuries.

The third priority, and perhaps the most costly in each local library, is the establishment of an actual program of restoration of selected editions of children's books. The selections must be made by the librarian so that only those which are deemed bibliographically, literarily, and historically significant receive high priority. This is a practical matter since at the present time the restoration process is costly. From the condition in which I find many of our children's books, I suspect that the restoration effort may have to precede the microfilming; but this is a curatorial detail. The important point is that individually and collectively we come to agreement on priorities and then act out our convictions.

PROCESS

Having established priorities, or at least the need for them, the librarian, the library, and the researcher must give consideration to the preservation process itself. The term 'process' as it is used here includes both the causes and the cures for deteriorating paper and books.

In oversimplified but alliterative terms, the process of preservation demands control—control of *people, pollution, pests,* and *poisons*!!

The literature of preservation and conservation has been sparse and sometimes hysterical but almost always it stresses the need for educating *people* to the need for careful and responsible handling of the book. The notion that a book is indestructible must be put to rest. This, of course, is not an inconsiderable task when dealing with the creatures for whom these particular books were originally intended. Our job would be much simpler if the children's book were made of hardened stainless steel sewed together with 5/8-inch cable. But the books will be used and some sadly abused. It is what remains when the book passes from active current use to archival status that must concern us. And it is these latter-day users who must learn that a book is a fragile thing, a thing which must be handled gently and treated delicately at every step.

An equally important provision is the need to educate the library staff to the dangers which may result from uninformed but well-intentioned efforts at repairing and maintaining older volumes. There is danger in the irreversibility of pressure-sensitive tape, the impurities in Elmer's glue; the sulphur contamination from rubber bands; and the chafing effect of paper clips. Often well-meant repairs become long-run problems for restoration.

If reader, researcher, and librarian will handle older children's books with care, the useful life of each book will be extended significantly, and there need be no crisis of access.

People obviously must have access to the books, but *pollutants* must be completely excluded from their contact with the collections. This is a difficult matter to accomplish in urban areas for it requires climate-control equipment and air-handling machinery which can filter gases as well as particulate matter from the air entering the library.

Then, in addition, there is the polluting effect from ultraviolet energy emitted by the sun as well as by fluorescent lamps. Fortunately, this polluting radiation can be filtered and books can be shielded. Properly-made boxes and neutral envelopes can save the day until the time when state and national environmental controls become more effective. The destructive effects of pollutants can be reduced if understood.

The eradication of *pests* is a third and vital element in the process of preservation, and it is a matter for continuing concern. The pests to which I refer here are the nonhuman creatures which devour our books more for the gelatin, glue, and fabric than for the literary content. Part of the battle against animal and insect pests is won with common cleanliness; part is won when foodstuffs are completely removed from areas in which books are used and stored; part is won when temperature and humidity are controlled and stabilized at about 68 degrees F. and 40 percent RH. But, victory is never complete, for every time another old book or reader enters the front door, pests can be among the uninvited guests.

And don't forget to include fungus and mildew in this category of unwanted pests. These latter organisms must be sought out and attacked rigorously, vigorously, and continuously. But, unlike the other pests, these, too, can be controlled and even eliminated with sanitary conditions, climate control, and with judicious use of fungicides, fumigants, and disinfectants.

People, pollutants, and pests can all be controlled and their damage to books limited. But the dangers which I have labeled *poisons* are much more difficult to limit and often much more costly to control. Actually, I must confess that the proper term which should be used to describe these materials is *acids*, but that word doesn't begin with the letter 'p'.

There are present in the paper-making process, in the sizing of paper, and in the general atmosphere the chemical ingredients and components of nitric, sulphurous, sulphuric, and hydrochloric acids. Under the generally varied climatic conditions of the average library, these acid ingredients attack the cellulose fibers, reduce their flexibility, and impair the durability and permanence of a sheet of paper as well as of the rigid structure of a book. The combined effects of these acids for the five-year period 1970 to 1975 has been cited by George Cunha as being more destructive than all the deterioration which occurred to books during the entire eighteenth century.

Not all paper used in publishing children's books is threatened with utter and complete destruction. Much of the eighteenth-century paper and that in the early part of the nineteenth century was generally made from clean rags and sized with gelatin. However, with the development in the nineteenth century of methods for making paper from less expensive wood fibers, and sizing with cheaper alum and resin, and with the introduction of increasing residues of chlorine bleaching materials, came the physical and chemical conditions for more rapid deterioration of paper and of books.

Every librarian is painfully familiar with badly hydrolized paper. It is often tan in color like weak coffee, parched-looking, extremely brittle, and almost completely unusable.

Although many of these sad cases are far gone and cannot be resurrected, many others can be saved. But it requires more than the simple idealism and desire of the good-hearted amateur. The trick is to introduce an alkaline solution into the cellulose fibers to neutralize the acids and to leave a residue of alkaline buffer to prevent the incursion of new molecules of acid.

This sounds somewhat like the Alka-Seltzer commercials, and surprisingly it is chemically similar. One of the common de-acidifying treatments for paper is to immerse it for at least one hour in a solution made from one or two Milk of Magnesia tablets dissolved in a quart of club soda. This is a simple cure for excess paper acidity as well as for human gastric disorders. This method was first reported and tested at the University of Chicago and has more recently been propagated by George Cunha of the New England Document Conservation Center. But, for more sophisticated and professional de-acidification much more is needed, including the talents, training, and experience of a professional conservator.

The acids, then, or poisons, can be neutralized and all the other hazards to books can be controlled—people, pollution, and pests. When these dangers are understood and controlled, the process of preservation will have been well begun.

PROBLEMS

So far, so good! We establish priorities. We become aware of the process! Why, then, isn't more being accomplished? There are a number of factors involved in answering this question, and these I label the problems of preservation.

The first problem, and one of the most difficult to overcome, is that of administrative reluctance. Administrators of large libraries are bombarded daily with hundreds of emergencies and numerous crises. The slow, quiet decay of a one-hundred-fifty-year-old children's book goes unnoticed. And, since all the collections of every library are deteriorating, the problem appears overwhelming, even to the most sensitive and concerned administrator. But few have the time or inclination to become concerned. Those who do are staggered by the extent of the problem and are stunned by the potential costs. Certainly, the costs by today's methods will be at least 50 percent of the book budget. It is probably this fact which is the most significant contributor to the existence of administrative reluctance.

A second, and perhaps more pervasive problem, is one which I call professional ignorance. I use the term *ignorance* to denote the state of *not knowing* rather than the condition of *stupidity*, although one is often a stage of the other. It is the ostrich principle which has dominated the library profession for many years with regard to the subject of preservation and conservation.

For example, no library school has yet made a long-term and consistent commitment to train the entering or the practicing professionals in their responsibilities for conservation. There have, of course, been a few bright spots. The University of Rhode Island Library School has offered a credit course on book and paper conservation for at least two semesters this past year. I have heard it said that Simmons College intends to offer a similar course, if indeed it has not already done so. This summer, the Library School at Columbia University is offering a course on library conservation to be taught by the Conservator of the Newberry Library, Paul Banks. This particular course has been created by Prof. Belanger and has been oversubscribed by 200 percent. In 1970, the University of Chicago Graduate Library School did a service for the profession when it published a number of excellent papers in Volume 40, Number 1 of the *Library Quarterly*. But, these bright spots are exceptions. The general practice of the professional schools has been to ignore this particular line of professional inquiry.

Worse still is that although neutral paper and stable materials for book-making have been available for years, the library profession has made no serious demands upon the publishing industry for their use. The paper being used today suffers from the same acid conditions as that made a hundred years ago. The Barrow Laboratory report on *Physical and Chemical Properties of Book Papers, 1507–1949* (Richmond, Va., 1974) states in part:

> Thus during the first half of this century [twentieth] little or no attention was paid to the production of permanent and durable book papers. Librarians and archivists are now living with the consequences.

We can only conclude that librarians have not read the literature on conservation, or have avoided the matter by ignoring it. It is more than likely that among our group gathered here in Boston this weekend, far more time and energy is given to problems of acquisition and circulation than is given to the vital question of conservation and preservation.

A third problem, and one which will be solved only in the course of time, is that of technical reticence. This phrase stands for a number of elements, but primarily to foot-dragging among conservation technicians. The state of the conservation art is mottled with confusion, doubt and uncertainty. For instance, a variety of materials and procedures are advertised in various places as promising aids for the cure of distressed paper and books. But, upon close examination, many of these cures have been inadequately tested or have been rushed to market to capture a few dollars. I think of one material which was being marketed two or three years ago under the name REGNAL. The literature promised great things, including quick and easy de-acidification and preservation of bound volumes of old newspapers. But, the actual experience from use of the material was something less than satisfactory.

To compound the problem further is the absence of agreed-upon professional standards for procedures and materials to be used in the restoration process. It is still an uncertain matter.

And nothing can be more uncertain right now than the prospect for a mass de-acidification process in our lifetime. The W. J. Barrow Laboratory has recently received additional support from the Council on Library Resources and the National Endowment for the Humanities for the development of a process for mass de-acidification using Morpholine vapor in a vacuum chamber. Yet Bernard Walker, the Director of the laboratory, reported that it would be mid-1977 before a test could be made under library conditions. And at almost the same time, there was re-published an old report which stated that Morpholine vapor was a relatively ineffective de-acidification agent. Does this suggest uncertainty?

At the Library of Congress, Frazer Poole reported recently that they were experimenting with a mass de-acidification process using Diethylzinc vapor. But only three years ago a film of this process was shown in which the conservator performed the treatment while an assistant in an asbestos suit stood by with firefighting equipment at the ready. The commentary stated that the process was slightly unstable!

Then consider the effort of Dr. Richard Smith, the inventor of Wei T'o Spray. Dr. Smith has been planning a mass de-acidification process for the Public Archives and National Library of Canada. In his plan he intends to use a magnesium methoxide non-aqueous process. After several years of planning, Dr. Smith reported recently that his work was still not ready for testing. And to compound that uncertainty, a patent has been recently awarded to a scientist, George Kelly, in the Preservation Research Office of the Library of Congress. The Kelly process is designed to use a methyl magnesium carbonate which is allegedly a more efficient and effective system of non-aqueous de-acidification than that designed by Smith.

To add to all this uncertainty, consider the hysteria which developed about five years ago over the Langwell Vapor-Phase process for mass de-acidification. At that time, the Langwell process was condemned in America because the cyclohexamine carbonate which it used was considered to be a dangerous carcinogen. But in February of this year, the Food and Drug Administration published the results of tests run by Dr. Elizabeth Weisburger which pronounced the Langwell process safe for library use.

There really is confusion resulting from the absence of technical decision-making among the practitioners. It is this technical reticence which creates many problems which must be solved if ever we librarians are going to do what has to be done.

The fourth problem is one which is difficult to assess and divisive in its effect. This one I call conservatorial arrogance. The leaders in the field of paper conservation snipe away at each other, criticize and carp, and add invective to professional uncertainty. This problem has a serious effect on those of us who are outside. It is a complex situation.

There is tension between conservators who have been trained at graduate schools versus those who have been trained at the bench and on the job. There is tension between conservators employed by institutions and those who are in private practice. There are conservators who believe that there should be certifying standards and licensing procedures and there are others who are violently opposed.

Regrettably, there is in all this a personal element, and evidence of ill will which distorts the truth and destroys some of the credibility of the profession. At a time when personal and professional cooperation is needed, very little is forthcoming. And this is a problem of some magnitude.

PROMISE

But the future is not all bleak. There is promise that we shall be able to preserve the early American children's books, which is our immediate concern. There are a number of suggestions that help is on the way.

One example is the Preservation Office of the Library of Congress. Under the competent direction of the Chief Preservation Officer, Peter Waters, leadership is being established, standards are being developed, and materials and processes are being tested.

Of equal stature is the work being undertaken in the Office of Museum Programs of the Smithsonian Institution. The Chief of Conservation, Mr. Robert Organ, has created a slide series and a video-tape series for education and in-service training of library preservation personnel. These materials also serve as excellent instructional aids for librarians, administrators, and trustees.

Closer to us here in Boston is the New England Document Conservation Center under the direction of George Cunha. The center provides not only the services of a restoration workshop, but also regularly offers training in the field of paper conservation in the form of a continuing education series for librarians, archivists, and conservational technicians, and all those who are concerned with the preservation of books and paper.

Somewhat more distant both in mileage and in mission is the testing function which is still being provided by the Barrow Research Laboratory in Richmond. It was their series of studies on the permanence and durability of the book which alerted librarians first to the destruction which was occurring in the stacks. The current programs of testing and publication of the Barrow Laboratory will continue to offer all of us the hard data which we need in order to help us make the decisions which must be made.

Finally on my list of promise for the future is the American Institute for Conservation, with its headquarters in Washington, D.C. The Executive Secretary, Charlotte Burk, oversees the distribution of regular publications which air and share most of the basic research which is being done in the field. In addition, the Institute conducts annual conferences which in themselves are highly technical training experiences for the expert and thorough instructions for the beginner.

There is promise in the work of these five organizations and institutions. There is also promise in the educational programs which are being supported or provided by a number of educational institutions throughout the country.

There is the Institute for the Conservation of Art at Oberlin; the Winterthur Program in Conservation at the University of Delaware; the Cooperstown Graduate Program in Conservation of the State University of New York at Oneonta; the Institute of Fine Arts at New York University; and the Fogg Museum Program in Conservation at Harvard. These programs, although primarily concerned with conservation of works of art, do produce techniques and procedures as well as a growing number of trained specialists who can and will do preservation work on paper and books.

With the priorities firmly established; with the process of preservation known and understood; with the problems of preservation overcome, the promise of the future for preserving the decaying remnant of the past may be realized before it is too late, after all. Then my little friend, Red Riding Hood, instead of being devoured by big bad ACID will live to tell her story over again from the pages of the eighteenth- and nineteenth-century children's books; and, once again Good will triumph over Evil as *Peter Parley picks priorities, participates in the process, perceives the problems, and pursues the promise of preservation.*

ADDENDUM TO RANDOM NOTES ON
THE PRESERVATION OF EIGHTEENTH- AND
NINETEENTH-CENTURY CHILDREN'S BOOKS

Five Sources of Information and Assistance On Problems of Preservation

1. Preservation Office—Administrative Department
   Library of Congress
   Washington, D.C. 20540
   > Of particular note is their series of leaflets *Preservation Leaflet Series*—1975. When completed it will include fourteen valuable guides to preservation.

2. Office of Museum Programs
   A & I Building—Room 2235
   Smithsonian Institution
   Washington, D.C. 20560
   > Note their program on *Conservation Information* which began in 1975. It includes a seven-program slide series and a sixty-program video-tape series for instruction and training.

3. New England Document Conservation Center
   800 Massachusetts Avenue
   North Andover, Massachusetts 01845
   > The Director and staff of this agency have produced a number of important reference works.
   > Cunha and Cunha, *Conservation of Library Materials* (1971).
   > Cunha and Tucker, *Library and Archives Conservation* (1972).
   > Morrison, Cunha, and Tucker, *Conservation Administration* (1975).

4. W. J. Barrow Research Laboratory, Inc.
   Virginia Historical Society Building
   428 North Boulevard
   Richmond, Virginia 23221
   > Their seven-volume series on *Permanence/Durability of the Book* (1963–1974) should be in the working collection of every librarian with a serious interest in the dimensions of the preservation problem.

5. American Institute for Conservation
   Executive Secretary
   1725 19th Street, N.W.
   Washington, D.C. 20009
   > A regular *Bulletin* and *Newsletter* as well as annual meetings provide much-needed and detailed information about a number of developments in the entire field of preservation and conservation.

8.
PECULIAR DIFFICULTY:
A TALE OF
THE EIGHTEENTH CENTURY

Being an Account
Of Some Lamentable Lacks,
Together with a Few Desperate Needs

GERALD GOTTLIEB

Peculiar difficulty: I am indebted for the phrase to Iona and Peter Opie, who used it in their introduction to the section on early children's books in the *New Cambridge Bibliography of English Literature*. They were referring to the problems of dating early children's books,[1] but the phrase describes marvelously what confronts us in a great many aspects of these books, apart from just their dates. If anything, the phrase is an understatement. For it is a melancholy fact that insufficient numbers of scholars have given insufficient amounts of attention to the problems of early children's books. And it is an even more melancholy fact that the supply of tools we have at present is woefully inadequate. (The second melancholy fact is of course a result of the first.) In her recent Anne Carroll Moore Lecture, Miss Virginia Haviland, Head of the Children's Book Section of the Library of Congress, remarked that she is seeing an upsurge of activity at the Library of Congress by scholars doing research in eighteenth-century children's books. I can report that the same thing is happening at the Pierpont Morgan Library. And it appears to be happening elsewhere as well. These are encouraging signs, certainly, but what do these scholars find when they attempt to investigate eighteenth-century children's books, particularly English children's books of the period? They find much darkness. If they try to make their way forward in almost any direction they soon find themselves halted for lack of a trustworthy guide. There is simply too much that we do not know. There are not enough tools, not enough bibliographies both basic and special, not enough dictionaries of all kinds, not enough studies great or small. Much is needed. Not enough questions are being answered. What is even worse, not enough questions are being asked. Everyone is aware by now that in the eighteenth century in England there were certain crucial, formative happenings in the development of the children's book. These happenings should not be allowed to remain dim to our eyes.

I should like to suggest a few things that might be done to help us, a few paths down which more light might be cast. The first need I will mention is something that would illuminate not just a path but in fact the whole forest. It is an eighteenth-century Short-Title Catalog. This is something that many bibliographers have categorized as an impossible dream, because the proliferation of books was simply too great after 1700—after, that is, the period of the Pollard and Redgrave Short-Title Catalog and the Wing Short-Title Catalog. (Eighteenth-century scholars have always regarded both these bibliographies with an intense, wistful longing.) The computer may now make it possible after all. It is on record that shortly after World War II, when the British government had acquired its first 'electronic brain,' as the computer was called then, a cabinet minister remarked, 'It isn't true, you know, that this is a great brain. We have to tell it the simplest things.' Well, the computer is now apparently capable of absorbing whatever complicated things we decide are necessary to discriminate among the variant issues of an eighteenth-century title, and we seem to be on our way toward a Short-Title Catalog of eighteenth-century books. If it does becomes a reality it will be vast, but it will be vastly useful. This will of course be an *enumerative* bibliography. If in my discussion of bibliographical needs I tend to stress this kind of approach, it is because I believe that the precise, systematic identifying and dating of editions, issues, and states is central to any study of the history of books and of their contents and influence, whether social, intellectual, or cultural. Sound bibliographical knowledge is the essential solid platform from which proper study should be launched.

The problems that can arise in matters of sequence—the stuff of enumerative bibliography—are perhaps obvious; but a great many other unhappy things can befall the scholar who is not bibliographically sophisticated. The first editions of some of the novels of Daniel Defoe offer a case in point. If one reads the title, and especially the long subtitle, of a Defoe work, and then goes on to read the book, a disparity is often evident that makes the novelist appear overhasty, careless, shoddy, and even venal. Frequently it seems that Defoe promises on the title page delights or excitements that he then does not bother to deliver. Sometimes he even can be seen to reverse in his text the political allegiance he displays on his title page. An instance of this is the novel

Colonel Jack, whose hero is depicted on the title page as a swashbuckling Jacobite rebel, whereas in the story he is made to be a rather more meek supporter of the king. This has been explained as an act of expediency on the part of Defoe, whose original intent—as shown by his title page—was to capitalize on romantic memories of the Rebellion, some years in the past. But then a new plot to overthrow the Crown was suddenly discovered, and public indignation flared up—whereupon the shifty novelist trimmed his sails to the prevailing wind. Analyses like this of a number of his novels and their title pages have gained Defoe a reputation for (depending on the novel) duplicity, avarice, or just shockingly bad artistry.

But the scholar with a bit more bibliographical knowledge would have a grasp of the real situation here. He would know that in the eighteenth century the title page of a novel generally owed its wording to the publisher, not the author. He would know that the title pages were often printed up in quantity and posted as advertisements, and that they usually exhibited in their wording all the scrupulousness we expect today from the publishers of, say, the paperback thrillers sold at the corner drugstore. Thus the titles found at the head of Defoe's books neither represent his own wording nor embody his own plan for the story. A great novelist has been defamed.[2]

Speaking of bibliographical sophistication, an exemplary study is William Sloane's *Children's Books in England and America in the Seventeenth Century*.[3] It is a full, sensitive, and wonderfully illuminating historical study, but it is also a bibliography firmly based on the sequences established by Pollard and Redgrave to 1640 and Wing to 1700. We need a study that does for the eighteenth century what this book does for the seventeenth. I hope such a study is being produced somewhere now; whoever does it could do worse than use the Sloane book as a model. (Incidentally, although I don't like to appear any more ignorant than is absolutely unavoidable, I'd love to be told that something I've suggested as a need is indeed being produced by someone this very moment—or in fact *was* produced only a month ago.)

We need more dictionaries of the eighteenth-century book trade, to help us identify the sometimes elusive publishers of these little books, and to tell us when they were active in their publishing and under what imprints. In this case, as it happens, I know of at least two dictionaries that are being worked on right now. One will cover the last quarter of the eighteenth century—the preceding three quarters being already covered by a group of books all brought out under the auspices of the Oxford Bibliographical Society.[4] And the extremely valuable list of publishers, booksellers, and printers which forms an Appendix to Volume I of Miss Judith St. John's Osborne Collection catalog is in process of being expanded and will appear in the next volume (III) of the catalog. Unlike the Bibliographical Society volumes, the Osborne list of course confines itself to the trade in children's books; it also is limited to names that appear in books in the Osborne Collection.

Compilations of this sort are enormously useful, but we also need studies of individual firms. It is hardly necessary for me to spell out here the value of Sydney Roscoe's tremendous bibliography of the books published by John Newbery and his successors.[5] It is a great achievement; and Mr. Roscoe is working on a supplement to make it even greater. But what about John Marshall, who between 1780 and 1800 was the principal rival of the Newberys in publishing for the juvenile market? And there is Edward Ryland, who in the 1760s produced such remarkably interesting, tasteful, and alas mysterious books as *The Bartholomew-Tide Fairing*, *The World Turned Up-Side Down*, *The Conjurer*, and *The Cries of London; or, Child's Moral Instructor*. And there is also Mary Cooper, who with the better-known Thomas Boreman antedates John Newbery as a publisher of children's books. And going back still further, there is of course Nat Crouch, known also as R. B., or Robert Burton, or Richard Burton, a bookseller-author (like John Newbery, though about half a century earlier) who is as mysterious as he is important. I can think of no better way to describe his importance than by quoting the estimable P. H. Muir on him: 'This enterprising and industrious hackney scribbler and bookseller seems to mark the first real effort to provide children with reading-matter—it is far from literature—to which they would look forward with pleasure and excitement in their leisure time.'[6] Our knowledge about Crouch comes principally from a fascinating, idiosyncratic autobiography entitled *The Life and Errors of John Dunton* (1705). Dunton, a bookseller, tells us just a little about Crouch; we need to know much more. We need to know much more about many others of these early publishers.

Taking a broader view, we need studies that will shed more light on the operations of the London and provincial English book trade in the eighteenth century. A fuller knowledge of publishers' congers, and of the sometimes complex arrangements for the transfer of copyright and the sale and distribution of children's books in this period would be of great help in the face of some of the puzzling imprints on the title pages of these books. And we could use help with more than just the title pages: Many of these books contain book lists, advertisements by the publisher of other books he has for sale. These lists were inserted in books from about the middle of the seventeenth century, but for various reasons the practice declined by the eighteenth century. represent an area of study that is fascinating, rewarding, and unfortunately full of pitfalls—almost as many pitfalls as lie in wait in the equally fascinating but even more slippery study of the advertisements publishers placed in newspapers and journals. 'This day is published . . .' the notices would begin. Pity the scholar faced with three such notices, all for the same title, all identically worded, thus giving him a choice of three dates of publication, spread over two or three years perhaps. How is he to decide on which—if any—of the three dates the book was actually published? We need more studies to help poor souls like him.

In investigating book lists and publishers' advertisements a good place to begin—and it is a good place to begin the study of quite a few book-trade matters—is Graham Pollard and Albert Ehrman's Roxburghe Club volume, *The Distribution of Books by Catalogue, from the Invention of Printing to A.D. 1800*. But this wide-ranging, invaluable work pays only the most fleeting attention to children's books. We need a thoroughgoing general study of the business of publishing books for children in the eighteenth century.

Now, what of the books themselves, these small, often endearing physical objects with their crude but charming woodcuts and their fragile wrappers of green gilt or Dutch flowered paper, or sturdy marbled boards backed with green vellum spines? Let us begin with their bindings. These are deserving of much more study. We are speaking now not of the bespoke or custom-tailored binding commissioned from his local binder by an eighteenth-century squire to encase the latest set of sheets sent him by his bookseller. Our concern is rather edition binding—those bindings, casings, wrappers, or other book clothing applied by the publisher issuing the book, and forming part of the book as offered for sale. A chronology of these binding styles would help in the dating of eighteenth-century children's books—always bearing in mind the confusions presented by the publishers' occasional practice of issuing earlier sheets in later bindings. The first important study of these matters was Michael Sadleir's *The Evolution of Publishers' Binding Styles* 1770–1900.[8] Sadleir, however, made only the most peripheral mention of children's books before 1800. He cited a Newbery circular, which may have been issued as early as 1761, extolling Newbery bindings 'in the vellum manner'—that is, in half vellum and paper boards. Sadleir marveled that this mode of binding was not widely adopted by publishers for another quarter of a century.[9] But he was writing in 1930; today we are aware of many mid-century examples of this style, which may indicate that the mode was more widely adopted, and earlier, than Sadleir knew. The matter needs investigating. Anyone looking into it should read Graham Pollard's essay, 'Changes in the Style of Bookbinding, 1550–1830,' published in *The Library* in 1956.[10] This is an erudite and awesomely broad study, and it is basic to any consideration of these matters, but it is almost totally silent on the edition-binding practices of children's book publishers in the eighteenth century. Similarly, William A. Jackson's 'Printed Wrappers of the Fifteenth to the Eighteenth Centuries,' published in the *Harvard Library Bulletin* in 1952,[11] is a study that the serious researcher will ignore at his peril—but in its discussion of the important distinctions among 'publisher's wrappers,' 'binder's wrappers,' 'integrated wrappers,' and 'wrap-arounds,' it touches hardly at all upon children's books of the eighteenth century.

The papers used for the wrappers and boarded bindings in which these children's books were issued—particularly the celebrated Dutch flowered and gilt papers—have attracted the attention of a few scholars. Rosamond B. Loring, in her *Decorated Book Papers* in 1942,[12] pointed out that these papers really were not Dutch but were German or Italian. They are of course familiar to us because they make appealing so many little volumes published for children in the eighteenth century, but they in fact go back much further than is generally realized. There is a record of their being exported from England to the American colonies in 1679. And—to add a final word on the matter—not all the Dutch papers were German or Italian. Some of them were English. In his *Styles and Designs of Bookbinding from the Twelfth to the Twentieth Century* (1956), Howard M. Nixon cites a book with a circa 1763 leather binding in the style known as 'Edinburgh floral' which has endpapers of a Dutch flowered paper that was manufactured in England.[13] And then there are marbled papers to consider. Some study has been made of their employment as endpapers in bespoke bindings, but there has been little or no study of the use of the same papers on the edition bindings of children's books, where they appear from at least 1750 onward. We need, in short, to know a lot more about all these paper matters.

The crude but charming woodcuts that I mentioned earlier are always rewarding to study. But any investigation tends to point up how little we know about the people who produced the cuts and engravings found in eighteenth-century children's books (apart, that is, from Thomas and John Bewick—but they were far from being the only practitioners of the art). We need studies of individual artists, and we need a comprehensive dictionary of the woodcutters and engravers whose work fills the children's books of our period. And the blocks themselves have histories that would tell us much, could they but be revealed. At the Morgan Library, for example, there is a copy—it is the only one known—of a circa 1772 Dublin edition of Christopher Smart's *Hymns, for the Amusement of Children*. It is illustrated with a series of woodcuts in the form of lovely oval headpieces. The Library also has a copy—it is one of only two that are known—

of the first American edition of the book, published in Philadelphia in 1791. It too is illustrated with woodcuts—and many of them were printed from the very same blocks used in the Dublin edition two decades earlier. No one, so far as I am aware, knows the circumstances of the transatlantic journey of these little blocks. There is work to be done here.[14] Ideally, what we need is a study that traces the migration of the woodblocks used in children's books in the eighteenth century—a work that would do for the period what Edward Hodnett did for an earlier time in his *English Woodcuts 1480–1535*,[15] or what R. B. McKerrow did in his *Printers' and Publishers' Devices in England and Scotland 1485–1640*.[16]

I have spoken of the papers used for the bindings of these early children's books. What of the paper on which they are printed? A thorough study of the watermarks in English and imported paper used in children's books of the period would be of great value in coping with the many undated imprints we have. Modern beta-radiograph techniques make such a study quite feasible now. A very useful but sketchy investigation—it is little more than a note—of some English papers that incorporate dates in their watermarks was made by C. B. Oldham in 1945. At first glance the existence of such dated watermarks would seem to be cause for rejoicing. But the investigator soon finds that extreme caution is required in assessing these apparently God-sent dates.[17] More study of the paper used in printing children's books in the eighteenth century is obviously needed.

And we also need to know more about the typography in these books. There is, for example, the question of type sizes. We accept as logical today that small readers should require large type. But this did not always seem obvious, as anyone knows who is at all familiar with the small-format, small-type volumes that were given to children in the first half of the eighteenth century. When did the change to larger typefaces take place? And who was responsible for it?

Then there is the enormously important matter of the physical makeup of the books we are considering, and the still not perfectly understood printing-house practices behind them. A proper comprehension of such things as final-text-page pastedowns and reset booklists is essential; we need studies of some of the ways in which the often ephemeral productions for children differ from the books produced for adults, to help us sort out the more bizarre printings and quirings confronting us. And to mention just in passing the matter of descriptive bibliography, or the specialized analytical language by which scholars exchange information about these books: Early children's books can present problems not easily solved by recourse to such standard authorities as McKerrow or Bowers or Gaskell. All efforts to attack these problems in a useful, systematic way are to be applauded. No one should attempt to approach them, incidentally, without first reading D. F. MacKenzie's provocative observations in his 'Printers of the Mind: Some Notes on Bibliographical Theories and Printing-House Practices,'[18] and also David Foxon's *Thoughts on the History and Future of Bibliographical Description.*[19]

Up to this point I have been considering our needs in terms of the printing and publishing of books for children in the eighteenth century. I should like now to conclude by casting before you a few random suggestions for studies that concentrate on what might be termed the intellectual aspects of these books—their themes, authors, compilers, adapters, illustrators, and of course their readers.

A few commendably penetrating studies of authors have been given us. Miss M. J. P. Weedon's classic presentation and analysis of the account books of Richard Johnson, the hack writer who was so prolific in his labors for the Newbery publishing enterprises, is a seminal work.[20] And the Oxford University Press Juvenile Library series, in which facsimile reprints are combined with bio-bibliographies, includes some studies that are noteworthy for their scholarship and for the light they shed on important writers. Mrs. Jill Grey's study of Sarah Fielding and *The Governess* is particularly fine, as are Mrs. M. Nancy Cutt's book on Mrs. Sherwood and J. H. P. Pafford's on Isaac Watts and his *Divine Songs.*[21] These are all admirable, but we need more like them, more author bibliographies, biographies, and bio-bibliographies. One hears that the Kilners, Dorothy and Mary Ann, are the subject of work in progress, but is anyone studying Mrs. Barbauld? Can someone tell us more about Benjamin Church, who wrote under the nom de plume of Thomas Thumb, Esq.? And the scholar who makes positive identifications of even some of the many children's books alleged to have been written by, or very probably written by, or usually attributed to, Oliver Goldsmith will be performing a service indeed.

Anonymous and pseudonymous works for children of course abound in the eighteenth century. We badly need studies of such concealed authorships, perhaps even full-scale dictionaries of anonyma, like Halkett and Laing or like the Barbier *Dictionnaire des ouvrages anonymes* for French works.

That the themes in eighteenth-century children's books merit serious study no one would deny. But how many scholars today are investigating such common themes in these books as the *commedia dell'arte*, or the noodle, or John Bull happiest by his own fireside, which possess, respectively, cultural, social, and historical significance? Proverbs, maxims, adages, and old wives' tales have always been an important ingredient in children's books. We need a study of them to put on the shelf beside Iona and Peter Opie's definitive study of nursery rhymes.[22] Emblem books have a rich and fascinating background. An investigation of those produced for children in the eighteenth century would be extremely useful.

Children's books embody adult social attitudes, and nowhere is this better displayed than in adaptations made for the young from works originally intended for their elders. Should we not have a study of such adaptations in the eighteenth century, which saw so many of them, from Defoe's *Robinson Crusoe* to Richardson's *Sir Charles Grandison*? The revolutions in America and France affected the world of eighteenth-century England in ways that historians are still pondering. Should we not have a study of the influence these social and political upheavals had on children's books? And has anyone measured their impact on the educational board games that were so popular in the era?

Everyone knows that chapbooks—street literature—were the underground in which were preserved the folklore and fairy tales that were officially unacceptable in eighteenth-century England. We need more studies of chapbooks as progenitors of children's literature. For that matter, we need to know more about the broadside ballads that preceded the chapbooks. These often carried pictures that were links in a chain that stretched from mediaeval manuscripts to eighteenth-century children's books.

Today the term 'children's book' almost automatically connotes pictures. But in the eighteenth century this was just beginning to be true. A study of the migration or descent of images from their origins in adult works that were the precursors of children's books would be most valuable. So would be a study of the development of pictorial themes as children's books evolved throughout the eighteenth century. And certainly the development of picture-assisted education, which was conceived some time before Comenius[23] and matured in the eighteenth century, should be fully charted for us.

The history of reading in the eighteenth century warrants more attention. J. H. Plumb has written with penetration about the reading fare of eighteenth-century children, and he is engaged now on a work that may tell us considerably more about childhood in that century, and about its preoccupations. But there is still much room for scholarly investigation of these matters. It is not just children's reading that merits attention, but adult reading as well. For example, there has been some study of John Locke's personal library,[24] but perhaps his library would bear revisiting in the light of what we now know about Locke's involvement in the anonymous illustrated Aesop of 1703—a children's book that embodies his philosophy of education.[25]

These random suggestions will hardly stimulate a massive onslaught upon all the many possible targets. But I should like to see such an onslaught, and I should like to see guides and indexes to the results someday. Perhaps there is in the offing something like *The Harvard Guide to American History*, or G. Thomas Tanselle's *Guide to the Study of United States Imprints*. And why not an annual review, a *Year's Work in Early Children's Book Studies*? One can hope, at least.

As a final word I should like to voice a *caveat*. Children's books in the eighteenth century, though they have a unique importance, are still part of a larger continuum. If new studies and bibliographies are to be made, they should recognize this fact. They should strive to establish the books in their proper context, to show why and how they developed as they did, to show the ways in which they relate to each other and to history. This may seem elementary, but experience has shown that the bibliographer can fall into a trap. He can think of himself as a sort of scientist, and proceed to put down his results so mechanically (in the name of science) as to lose the larger vision. But for all my talk of computers and beta-radiographs, bibliography is not a science but an art, as medicine is in the end an art. The sophisticated bibliographer, like the best of physicians, will keep the whole organism in mind, no matter how absorbed he becomes in our 'peculiar difficulty.'

♁ ♁ ♁ ♁ ♁

(*At this point the discussion was opened with questions addressed to the three previous speakers.*)

(*Question concerning eighteenth-century French books.*)

GOTTLIEB: The English have studied eighteenth-century French books in some ways perhaps even more thoroughly than have the French themselves; so in many works, particularly journal articles by English scholars, you will find investigations of eighteenth-century French books, especially of what I refer to as the progenitors of children's books. For example, Percy Muir has written on the extensive influence of Rousseau on the French children's book. And there have been quite a few writings on Arnaud Berquin and *The Children's Friend*. Here again, as often happens in eighteenth-century children's books, a Continental work has had an important influence on English books.

(*Comment from the floor on perfect binding as being one of the less desirable ways in which to bind a book permanently.*)

BAUER: I highly agree. I would also agree that oversewing is perhaps the second most disastrous way of binding, which is the way that all periodicals are being bound by the commercial houses. The oversewing process does not allow the flexibility in the spine which it really needs to be opened, used, and copied. The perfect binding is just a glued binding. A remainder house is currently announcing a re-issue of the Isaiah Thomas *History of Printing in America* and saying it is the same edition that was sold for forty dollars. It is not. It is a cheaply-bound edition. We have received letters of complaint, although we have no control over the production of it. I guess it is going to take a major consumer protest to make an impact on binders. I wish we could unite, make placards, and parade in front of those publishing houses which allow this type of binding. I tried to organize the librarians at Worcester in demanding better binding practice, but they were uninterested, since they had bigger problems to solve. I think the question is nevertheless appropriate. We have to solve this problem in binding.

PARTICIPANT: *Can you tell us a little about the scope of the collections of early children's books at The Morgan Library?*

GOTTLIEB: We are back where I started, speaking about non-existent things. The nonexistent thing in this case is bibliographic control in the Morgan collections, which are almost entirely uncataloged. I am referring principally to the early children's books in the collection given us by Elisabeth Ball about a decade ago. These are not yet cataloged. There are, of course, as I tried to show in the exhibition and catalog last year, many ancestors, precursors, progenitors of these books in the previous holdings of The Morgan Library, going back to the earliest known papyrus manuscripts of Aesop's fables, and these are cataloged; but the Elisabeth Ball collection itself is uncataloged, and trying to find something is quite an adventure. What bibliographic control there is resides in the very imperfect memory of the curator himself. Also, we are in the process of building a new wing on The Morgan Library, with the result that the children's books have been moved two or three times, which further complicates our problem of bibliographic control. Scholars are becoming very familiar with that misty, somewhat terrified look I get when they ask me where something is, even something that was in the catalog of the exhibition.

You asked about the scope of the holdings. We are strongest in the eighteenth century—the English eighteenth century; we also have quite a few Continental things, again more eighteenth century than contemporary; and with considerable strength in French language works. We do have a very fine, but rather small, American collection put together by Gillett Griffin of Princeton University, and before him by Wilbur Macey Stone. This comprises about a thousand volumes. The uncataloged books in the Elisabeth Ball Collection come to at least twelve thousand items; and when you consider that the exhibition had slightly more than three hundred items in it, you see that we have only begun to scratch the surface. If I may say one more thing about the scope of the collections at the Morgan: In response to my own curiosity, and a lot of questions, I've made spot checks over the past two years or so, and the results are unbelievable, but I might as well tell you. It seems to be a fact that something more than 20 percent of our pre–nineteenth-century titles, rather better than one in every five, possibly one in every four, are unrecorded anywhere, or exist in a single unique copy at The Morgan Library. This is a sobering thought when you consider the amount of work this means; but it's a challenging thought, too.

NOTES

1. See George Watson, ed., *The New Cambridge Bibliography of English Literature*, 2: col. 1013–16, 1660–1800 (Cambridge: Cambridge University Press, 1971).

2. For some unjustified inferences that have been drawn from discrepancies between title page and text in Defoe's works, see Rodney M. Baine, 'The Evidence from Defoe's Title Pages,' in *Studies in Bibliography*, 25(1972):185–91.

3. William Sloane, *Children's Books in England and America in the Seventeenth Century* (Oxford: Kings Crown Press, 1955).

4. The dictionary of the period from 1775 to 1800 is being prepared for the Society by Ian Maxted.

5. Sidney Roscoe, *John Newbery and His Successors, 1740–1814: A Bibliography* (Wormley, Hertfordshire: Five Owls Press, 1973).

6. Percy Muir, *English Children's Books 1600 to 1900* (London: Batsford, 1954), p. 35.

7. Graham Pollard and Albert Ehrman, *The Distribution of Books by Catalogue, From the Invention of Printing to A.D. 1800* (Cambridge: printed for the Roxburghe Club, 1965).

8. Michael Sadleir, *The Evolution of Publisher's Binding Styles 1770–1900* (London: Constable, 1930).

9. Ibid., pp. 11–12.

10. *The Library*, Fifth Series, 11(1956):71–94.

11. *Harvard Library Bulletin*, 6(1952):313–21.

12. Rosamund B. Loring, *Decorated Book Papers* (Cambridge, Massachusetts: Harvard College Library Department of Printing and Graphic Arts, 1942), pp. 49–61.

13. Howard M. Nixon, *Styles and Designs of Book Binding—From the Twelfth to the Twentieth Century* (London: Published for the Broxbourne Library by Maggs Brothers, 1956), pp. 180–81.

14. See my *Early Children's Books and Their Illustration* (New York: Pierpont Morgan Library, 1975), pp. 165–166 and 168.

15. Edward Hodnett, *English Woodcuts 1480–1535* (Oxford: Bibliographical Society, 1935).

16. R. B. McKerrow, *Printers' and Publishers' Devices in England and Scotland 1485–1640* (London: Bibliographical Society, 1913).

17. C. B. Oldham, 'Watermark Dates in English Paper,' *The Library*, Fourth Series, 25(1945):70–71. The repeal in 1811 of the Excise Act of 1794 established clear reasons for mistrusting the dates of English papers watermarked 1811, but some eighteenth-century-dated watermarks also give rise to suspicion today.

18. *Studies in Bibliography*, 22(1969):1–75.

19. David Foxon, *Thoughts on the History and Future of Bibliographical Description* (Los Angeles: University of California School of Library Service, 1970).

20. Miss M. J. P. Weedon, 'Richard Johnson and the Successors to John Newbery,' *The Library*, Fifth Series, 4(1949):25–63.

21. Jill E. Grey, ed., *Sarah Fielding: The Governess, or Little Female Academy* (London: Oxford University Press, 1968).

M. Nancy Cutt, *Mrs. Sherwood and Her Books for Children* (London: Oxford University Press, 1974).

J. H. P. Pafford, ed., *Isaac Watts: Divine Songs Attempted in Easy Language for the Use of Children* (London: Oxford University Press, 1971).

22. Iona and Peter Opie, eds., *The Oxford Dictionary of Nursery Rhymes* (Oxford: Oxford University Press, 1951).

23. The Couvay brothers of Arles in southern France may have inspired Comenius; they at least preceded him in using techniques for which he is celebrated. See my *Early Children's Books and Their Illustration*, p. 99.

24. See John Harrison and Peter Laslett, eds., *The Library of John Locke* (Oxford: Oxford Bibliographical Society Publications, N.S., 1965); and also see Richard Ashcraft, 'John Locke's Library: Portrait of an Intellectual,' in *Transactions of the Cambridge Bibliographical Society*, 5, pt. 1 (1969): 47–60.

25. For a brief outline of the problem see my *Early Children's Books and Their Illustration*, p. 9; and for information that has more recently come to light, see Robert H. Horwitz and Judith B. Finn, 'Locke's Aesop's Fables,' in *Locke Newsletter*, 5 (Summer 1975): 71–88.

9.
MANUSCRIPTS OF
CHILDREN'S LITERATURE
IN THE BEINECKE LIBRARY

MARJORIE G. WYNNE

The first catalog of the library of Yale College was compiled by President Thomas Clap and printed in 1743, just forty-two years after the Collegiate School, as it was originally called, had been founded by ten Congregational clergymen meeting together in Branford, Connecticut. The 1743 catalog listed about twenty-five hundred books, mainly on theology, and students were cautioned in the introduction 'to have an Eye to the great end of all your studies, which is to obtain the Clearest Conceptions of Divine Things.' The library's *last* printed catalog appeared in 1823 and included among its sixty-six hundred titles at least one book that is sometimes considered suitable for children: Daniel Defoe's *Robinson Crusoe.*

During the next hundred and fifty years the Yale Library grew from six thousand to six *million* volumes and in the process acquired—inevitably but not always deliberately—an impressive number of books and manuscripts designed especially for children as well as a score of hornbooks, dozens of playing cards, hundreds of English and American chapbooks, and thousands of magazines and comic books.

Yale has a respectable collection of eighteenth-century manuscripts but none written for children, so far as I can discover. A hundred or so letters by Maria Edgeworth, including a few to Mrs. Barbauld, would certainly interest the historian, but even more interesting perhaps would be the evidence of Miss Edgeworth's influence on a particular child of a later generation.

John Ruskin was born in 1819, when Maria Edgeworth's fame had spread from Great Britain to Europe and America. 'My calf milk of books was,' he wrote in *Praeterita*, 'on the lighter side, composed of *Dame Wiggins of Lee*, the *Peacock at Home*, and the like nursery rhymes, and on the graver side, of Miss Edgeworth's *Frank*, and *Harry and Lucy*, combined with Joyce's *Scientific Dialogues*.' The fresh and felicitous mixture of entertainment and instruction found so generously in Miss Edgeworth's books was irresistible to the young Ruskin. At the age of seven or eight he filled several small notebooks with imitations of his favorite author and was, in fact, such 'a little Edgeworthian gosling,' as he later referred to himself, that he even called one of his own stories 'Harry and Lucy.'

In Ruskin's 'Harry and Lucy,' written in a fine copperplate hand, he described the life of an impossibly obedient and grown-up little boy whose absorbing curiosity about art, science, and nature would characterize Ruskin himself throughout a long and studious life. He instructed the imaginary Lucy in the names of the constellations, performed simple scientific experiments for her benefit, and illustrated the whole with innumerable little sketches of mountains, boats, houses, rabbits, and even silkworms.

When Ruskin was twenty-one years old he wrote a fairy story that would become his most popular book; he wrote it to amuse a very young lady who was visiting his family, as well as, perhaps, to prove that he could think of something besides minerals and arches. The young lady was Euphemia Gray, whom he married eight years later, and the story was *The King of the Golden River*, which was first published in 1850. *The King of the Golden River* was written in two or three sittings and apparently without effort, for the manuscript, now in the Beinecke Library, is neat and clean, with very few corrections. It was bought about forty years ago to add to the splendid collection of Ruskin first editions, manuscripts, letters, and drawings given to us in 1929 by R. B. Adam of Buffalo, New York.

We have no manuscripts by the poet and artist Edward Lear, but we do have several of his letters, some with amusing illustrations. In one, written from San Remo in 1872, he told his correspondent that he would like to send back a live elephant who could be 'taught to clean the windows beautifully,' and at the end of the letter, there is the sketch of the elephant scrubbing a lofty window with a sponge at the end of its trunk. In a letter of 1870 he enclosed nine drawings of nonsense flowers—Multipeoplea Upsidownia and Pollybirdia Singularis, among them—that are similar to those published the next year in his *Nonsense Songs, Stories, Botany, and Alphabets*.

Several years ago we were given a mid-nineteenth-century edition of the letters of Horace Walpole. On the endpapers of volumes 8 and 9 we were delighted to find the working manuscript of one of Lear's best-known poems, 'Incidents in the Life of My

Uncle Arly.' Here we see the author at work: trying various rhymes, inventing nonsense words, and even drawing a picture of Uncle Arly with the cricket on his nose, the ticket in his hat, and the shoes that were far too tight.

Another Victorian artist and poet who occasionally turned his talents to the amusement and edification of children was William James Linton. Linton was perhaps best known for his wood engravings, of which his illustrations to Moxon's Tennyson are among his most successful, but he was also a radical political reformer and the author of books about two other well-known radicals, Thomas Paine and Giuseppe Mazzini. Linton came to America in 1866 and settled in Hamden, Connecticut, just outside New Haven. He installed a hand press in his house and called it Appledore, and there for the next thirty years he printed a great many poems, pamphlets, circulars, and broadsides. Many of these, in multiple copies and varying states, were given to Yale after Linton's death in 1897, and among them are the manuscripts of two charming pieces: *Children's Songs* and *The Flower and the Star*. The manuscript of the first is illustrated with pencil and watercolor drawings, while the second is accompanied by page proofs containing rough pulls of cuts by Linton that do not appear in the printed version. There is also a little book of wild flowers found around Brantwood, the home on Lake Coniston that he sold to John Ruskin; the flowers are sketched and colored by Linton, with rhyming descriptions in his hand, all done for his daughter Elizabeth on her second birthday in 1856.

George MacDonald was a Scottish preacher, poet, mystic, dreamer, dramatist, novelist, lecturer, and actor who was idolized in his own day but is generally neglected in ours. We have no manuscripts of his books that children used to read and love (perhaps some still do)—*At the Back of the North Wind, The Princess and the Goblin, The Princess and Curdie*—but we do have a collection of MacDonald family papers that will be of the first importance in any future accounts of MacDonald's life and works.

There are nine hundred letters from MacDonald, mainly to his wife and children, written between 1837 and 1905; seven hundred seventy letters from Mrs. MacDonald to her husband; and eleven hundred seventy letters from the MacDonald children to their parents. There are also photograph albums, genealogical records, clippings about MacDonald's brilliant lecture tour in America in 1872–73, and printed dramatic versions of *Pilgrim's Progress* and *Blue Beard* prepared by Mrs. MacDonald and performed by members of the family and their friends.

The friends of the MacDonald family were numerous and interesting, and one of the most interesting was Lewis Carroll. He wrote delightfully imaginative letters to the MacDonald daughters and cherished their friendship even as they began to grow up. His genius as a correspondent and his happy relationship with the children are seen in passages like this: 'It's been so frightfully hot here,' he wrote to one of them on 23 May 1864, 'that I've been almost too weak to hold a pen, & even if I had been able, there was no ink—it had all evaporated into a cloud of black steam, & in that state it has been floating about the room, inking the walls & ceiling till they're hardly fit to be seen: today it is cooler, & a little has come back into the ink bottle in the form of black snow—there will soon be enough for me to write & order those photographs your Mamma wants.'

On 14 November 1864 he told Mary that he had been expecting the sonnet by Mr. Rossetti that she had promised to copy out and send, but 'post after post went by, & no sonnet came—I leave off here to explain how they sent letters in those days: there were no gates, so the gate-posts weren't obliged to stay in one place— consequence of which they went wandering all over the country— consequence of which, if you wanted to send a letter anywhere, all you had to do was to fasten it on to a gate-post that was going in the proper direction—(only they sometimes changed their minds, which was awkward)—This was called "sending a letter by the post."'

Mary's failure to answer one of his letters finally drew this anguished protest dated 13 March 1869: 'I wrote . . . on the 26th of January last, offering you a copy of the German edition of "Alice". Well, the days rolled on—and the nights too (as nearly as I can remember, one between every two days, or thereabouts), and *no answer* came. And the weeks rolled on, & the months too, & I got older & thinner, & sadder, and still *no answer* came.

And then my friends said—how white my hair was getting, & that I was all skin & bone, & other pleasant remarks—and— but I won't go on, it is too dreadful to relate, except that, through all these years & years of waiting & anxiety (all of which have elapsed since the 26th of January last—you see, we live so fast at Oxford) still *no answer* ever came from this granite-hearted young person! And then she calmly writes & says, "Oh, do come & see the race!" And I answer with a groan "I *do* see the race—the human race—it is a race *full of ingratitude*—& of all that race none is more ungratefuller, more worser—more—" my pen chokes, and I can say no more!'

There are twenty-five letters like this, all equally quotable, and several photographs of the children taken by Lewis Carroll. Other MacDonald family friends, some of whose letters are in the collection, are Matthew Arnold, Robert Browning, Octavia Hill, Charles Kingsley, and John Ruskin.

In 1858, at the age of thirteen, Walter Crane, the son of a provincial portrait painter, was apprenticed to the engraver, William James Linton. He emerged from this association with a lifelong respect for Linton, whom he saw on a trip to America in 1891–92; the seeds of socialism; and a skill in design that would lead him to preeminence as an illustrator of books and a designer of wallpapers, ceramics, embroideries, textiles, furniture, and stained glass.

Crane's best-known work is found in the toy-books produced in collaboration with the printer Edmund Evans and published by Routledge from 1865 to 1875. He illustrated dozens of fairy tales—*Cinderella*, *Beauty and the Beast*, *Bluebeard*, and *The Forty Thieves*—with spirit, elegance, and a richness of decorative detail that captivated children, and he wrote and illustrated humorous and imaginative books like *Pothooks & Perseverance* and *Slateandpencilvania*, in which little boys charged into battle with arithmetic and grammar.

For his own children, Lancelot, Lionel, and Beatrice, Crane drew nightly stories—one page a night for each child—and at least one of these, *Legends for Lionel*, was published by Cassell in 1887. Several others, apparently unpublished, are in the Beinecke Library. 'The House that Art Built,' 'Time's Show,' and

'Lancelot's Levities' display a marvelous sense of humor at the same time that they show the children how, for example, Art, with nothing to begin with but a flint knife and a few pieces of bone, eventually discovered the pointed arch and even invented a character named 'Flamboyant.'

The Walter Crane collection was given to us in 1956 by Mrs. Catharine Tinker Patterson, sister of Yale's Keeper of Rare Books, Chauncey Brewster Tinker. To mark the occasion of this gift an exhibition was opened with an address by Anthony Crane, grandson of the artist, and with the publication in facsimile of one of the children's manuscripts. This was *Mr. Michael Mouse unfolds his Tale*, an engaging story of the nineteenth-century predecessor of Mickey Mouse who, by the way, was invited to the opening of the exhibition and who said, in sending his regrets, how very pleased he was to discover his aristocratic ancestor.

Walter Crane did other things besides draw pictures for children: he painted pictures (the most famous of which is probably 'Neptune's Horses'); he was Principal of the Royal College of Art in South Kensington; he wrote books on the theory of art; and he also illustrated other people's books, including two by Robert Louis Stevenson, *An Inland Voyage* and *Travels with a Donkey*.

Yale's Stevenson collection, probably the largest of its kind, was formed by Edwin J. Beinecke and given to us in 1951. In addition to first and early editions of all the books, there are hundreds of letters to and by Stevenson (some to his parents when he was still a child), and the manuscripts of many of his poems, essays, stories, and novels.

In 1880, when Stevenson was thirty years old, he married an American divorcée with a twelve-year-old son named Lloyd Osbourne. Lloyd accompanied the Stevensons on their honeymoon in California and later went with them to Switzerland, where RLS hoped to find a congenial climate. One of the toys that Lloyd brought along was a very small printing press, and Stevenson threw himself into the productions of this press with all the enthusiasm of a man caught in a prolonged adolescence. He wrote poems like 'Not I,' two stanzas of which are:

Some like drink
  In a pint pot,
Some like to think,
  Some not.

Some like Poe,
  And others like Scott,
Some like Mrs. Stowe;
  Some not.

And when illustrations were called for, he used a penknife and
then a graver to cut wood blocks. He gave testimonials to the
young printer and author of a wild west story called *Black Canyon*—'A very remarkable work. Every page produces an effect.
The end is as singular as the beginning. I never saw such a work
before'—and generously helped with the production of a series
of miniature poems, stories, newspapers, and advertisements.
The manuscripts of many of these poems are in the Beinecke
Library, some unpublished, along with a few of Stevenson's wood
blocks and wood-cutting tools.

Three years after these trifles for a toy press Stevenson had a
more substantial collection of children's poems ready for publication. He selected forty-eight and had them printed in a twenty-
two-page pamphlet headed *Penny Whistles* (there was no cover
and no title page). Only three copies of *Penny Whistles* are
known to have survived, and the one in the Beinecke Library is
particularly interesting because of its marginal notes by Sidney
Colvin and William Ernest Henley, two friends who were asked
to comment on the poems before they were actually published.

Six poems were discarded on the joint recommendation of
Colvin and Henley, and three more were thrown out by Stevenson himself. Neither Colvin nor Henley liked 'A Good Boy,'
both used their delete signs, and Colvin added 'priggish,' but it
remained; Colvin wanted to drop 'The Lamplighter'—'an extinct
animal to the modern child'—but Henley liked it, and it was
kept. Colvin said that 'How do you like to go up in a swing/Up in
the air so blue' was commonplace, but Henley crossed out that
remark with a flourish, and the poem stayed. Neither Colvin nor

Henley liked 'The Birthday Party' (Colvin said he had read almost the same lines on Christmas crackers) and it was discarded. In 1885 the remaining thirty-nine poems, and twenty-five new ones, were published by Longmans, Green and Co. as *A Child's Garden of Verses*, and we have the working manuscripts of most of them.

If Stevenson could say of himself when his resemblance to Shelley was suggested, 'a Shelley with less will and no genius, though I have had the fortune to live longer and (partly) to grow up,' J. M. Barrie will probably always be identified with the boy who *never* grew up. Barrie's involvement with the character of Peter Pan covered almost three decades and is well-documented in the voluminous collection of books, manuscripts, letters, clippings, and pictures given to Yale by Walter Beinecke, Jr.

Peter Pan first appeared in Barrie's prose work *The Little White Bird*, of which we have the manuscript dated December 1901 and the galley proofs of the version serialized in *Scribner's Magazine* in 1902. Two years later, on December 27, the play called *Peter Pan* was produced at the Duke of York's Theatre in London. In 1906, six chapters from *The Little White Bird* were illustrated by Arthur Rackham and published separately as *Peter Pan in Kensington Gardens*. In 1911 a prose narrative of the play was published with the title *Peter and Wendy*, and finally the first edition of *Peter Pan*, as the world now knows it, was published in 1928.

Yale has Barrie's manuscript notes for the play (1903), several leaves of an early version, typescripts of three or four versions of the play (some with manuscript revisions and interleaved with lighting plots and stage business), the manuscript of an epilogue with a note by Hilda Trevelyan (the first Wendy) explaining how the play was written and produced, a scenario for a proposed film in 1920, the dedication 'To the Five,' various speeches and stories by Barrie relating to Peter Pan, and finally the manuscript of the play with this inscription on the flyleaf: 'M.S. of Peter Pan. The only one in existence so far as I know, to Cynthia Asquith from her affectionate J. M. Barrie. Dec. 1928. There are many alterations in the work as published.'

In addition to material tracing the evolution of the play, there are other assorted items that bear on its history and illustrate its popularity: letters to Nina Boucicault and Maude Adams (the first English and American Peter Pans), a deck of playing cards for a game called 'Peter Pan,' Arthur Rackham's original illustrations for *Peter Pan in Kensington Gardens*, notes describing the design of a special curtain to be used in the 1908 production, a letter from Barrie to Edmund Caley giving him permission to produce Peter Pan crackers with appropriate quotations on them, and the key to Kensington Gardens presented to Barrie by the City of London.

'The Five,' to whom the play was dedicated, were the five Llewelyn Davies boys whom Barrie beguiled with stories and games and whom he unofficially adopted after the early deaths of their parents. In the summer of 1901 three of the boys spent a holiday at the Barries' summer cottage on Black Lake in Surrey, and while the children were investigating the lake shore (changed into an imaginary South Seas lagoon) or exploring the pinewoods (tropical forests alive with enemies) Barrie took dozens of photographs of the young pirates. He selected thirty-five of the most successful, printed a title page and preface, and captioned each murky scene of white-suited little boys with the kind of heading usually found in stories of high adventure: 'A Fearful Hurricane,' 'We go Crazy from Want of Food,' 'We are Attacked by Wolves,' 'Jack saves George's Life,' and so on. The title given to this story is *The Boy Castaways*, and on the flyleaf of our copy Barrie wrote: 'There was one other copy of this book only and it was lost in a railway train in 1901. J.M.B. 1933.'

These, then, are some of our major resources for studying children and literature; in addition, we have innumerable manuscripts of fairy stories by Ethel May Gate, a fourteenth-century manuscript of Aesop's Fables, the typescript of A. A. Milne's dramatic version of Kenneth Grahame's *The Wind in the Willows*, and letters by Kate Greenaway, Thomas Hughes, Andrew Lang, Frances Hodgson Burnett, and Rosemary Benét.

Most of the large collections were given to us by alumni or other friends (the MacDonald collection was purchased in 1971). In accepting such gifts the library also accepts the responsibility for maintaining the collections in good condition, for adding to them whenever possible, and for making them available to all qualified scholars.

So far the Beinecke Library has ample space in temperature-and-humidity-controlled stacks for the storage of all of its manuscripts. Damaged manuscripts are repaired whenever possible; letters and other unbound manuscripts are put in acid-free folders and then stored in boxes on shelves or in filing cabinets; and bound manuscripts stand on shelves, sometimes in the custom-made boxes in which they arrived, sometimes in boxes or portfolios made to order by our Conservation Studio.

Additions to collections are made when both funds and manuscripts are available. We bid at auction and buy from dealers, but every purchase depends on the cost of the material in relation to its potential research value. We have been able to buy many important Stevenson and Barrie manuscripts because of generous support from the two members of the Beinecke family who gave us the original collections.

Scholars come from several continents to use this material, or else they write asking for photocopies! The Lewis Carroll letters in the MacDonald collection have been included in the collected edition of Carroll's letters now in press, and an article about the MacDonald papers will soon appear in our library *Gazette*, with special emphasis on the misuse of the letters by Greville MacDonald in writing the biography of his parents. A member of the faculty of the University of Calgary has just written asking permission to use the collection in the preparation of a critical study of MacDonald's fiction, especially his romances and children's books.

Isobel Spencer's new biography of Walter Crane (London: Studio Vista, 1975) made particular use of our unpublished stories for Beatrice, Lionel, and Lancelot. The late James Pope-Hennessy twice visited our collection before writing his biography of Robert Louis Stevenson, and a scholar in London is now editing all of Stevenson's letters for the Yale University Press. A distinguished psychoanalyst in New York has been up several times to study the diaries in which Stevenson's mother recorded the earliest words and deeds of her infant son.

Janet Dunbar's *J. M. Barrie. The Man Behind the Image*

(Boston: Houghton Mifflin, 1970) used unpublished material in our Barrie collection, and a Ph.D. candidate in London has asked for and received photocopies of the pertinent Barrie manuscripts and typescripts for a dissertation on fiction and fantasy in late nineteenth- and early twentieth-century children's literature, with special reference to the textual evolution of *Peter Pan*.

BBC Television is preparing a trilogy of fifty-minute plays about the life of Barrie, and their editors are using copies of the photographs in *The Boy Castaways*. Nothing could be more suitable for televised episodes relating to Barrie and the Davies boys than the pictures he took of them in the midst of their desert-island fantasy.

The Yale University Library may never have intended to collect manuscripts of children's literature, but in one way or another we have assembled an interesting array of material that has been used and *is* being used to discover what children in this century and the last wrote when they *were* children and, after they grew up, what they wrote for other children.

10.

LOST INNOCENCE
IN THE AMERICAN COMICS

WALTER SAVAGE

The thirty-second letter in Samuel Richardson's *Pamela* is sent by the heroine, a young, naive, and nubile maiden, to her parents, John and Elizabeth Andrews. Like most of those preceding it, it is about Pamela's beleaguered virginity, once more melodramatically imperiled by the attack of her employer and oppressor, Mr. B. In this particular letter, however, Pamela's 'vartue,' as Fielding was to call it, was threatened by not only the 'artful wiles of her wicked master,' but also Mrs. Jewkes, his housekeeper whom Pamela describes as 'a wicked procuress . . . that seems to delight in filthiness . . . a broad, squat, pursy *fat thing*, quite ugly, with a huge hand . . . an arm as thick as my waist . . . a hoarse man-like voice . . . a heart more ugly than her face . . .'[1] Jewkes, after watching Pamela undress, gets into bed with her and draws Pamela close to her side so that, Jewkes says, 'they can make room for Nan,' another serving girl who will later join them. Then Jewkes pinions Pamela's arms and calls to Nan, who slips in beside Pamela. Almost at once Pamela makes the terrifying discovery that 'Nan' is Mr. B. in disguise.

Richardson continues Pamela's account as follows: '. . . He kissed me with frightful vehemence and then his voice broke upon me like a clap of thunder. Now, Pamela, said he, is the dreadful time of reckoning come that I have threatened . . . I screamed out . . . but there was nobody to help me; and both my hands were secured . . . sure never poor soul was in such agonies as I . . . oh God! My God! This time! This one time! Deliver me from this distress! Or strike me dead this moment! . . . said [Jewkes] . . . What you do, sir, do; don't stand dilly dallying. She cannot exclaim worse than she has done; and she'll be quieter when she knows the worst. Silence! said he to her. I must say one word to you Pamela! You see you are in my power! . . . You cannot get from me, nor help yourself . . .'[2]

In such scenes Richardson presented a character and a situation that were to appear and re-appear almost endlessly and in innumerable forms and guises in Anglo-American fiction. Indeed, the image he flashed before his readers was to become in America, as well as in Britain, a cultural icon symbolizing a dark, recurring fantasy, dreadful but titillating, about the martyred victims of vile lust or pitiless domination.

Significant as she may have been as a catalyst initiating one of literature's most widely noted reactions, Pamela—flattened, spread-eagled, and writhing with hurt and helpless whimpers in that dim and isolated Lincolnshire bedroom—is equally important as model for emulation and monitory sexual metaphor. She is, as Utter and Needham note in *Pamela's Daughters*, 'very young, very inexperienced, and so delicate in physical and mental constitution that she faints at any sexual advance.'[3] She is a decarnalized creature, Ian Watt agrees in *The Rise of the Novel*, totally immune from sexual feelings, 'reserved for higher things,' in particular the disciplining of the unregenerate Adam in man, whose concupiscence Defoe saw as linking them with the one great source of evil, the devil himself: '"In our general pursuit of the sex, the devil generally acts the man . . ."'[4]

If 'My Favorite Erotic Experience,' an article in the April 1975 issue of *Cosmopolitan* reveals anything more than Helen Gurley Brown's editorial knowledge of what will play in Peoria, it suggests that the image of innocence beset retains its metaphorical and symbolic resonances for a fairly large American audience. Responding to a question put to twenty women concerning their 'most cherished erotic experience,' V. E., 'Secretary, Milwaukee, Wis.,' cited this conjugal encounter: 'My brand-new husband— we'd only been married three months—suddenly grabbed me and tied me to the bed posts one night. I was absolutely helpless— I couldn't move at all because my arms were spread-eagled. Then he went to work on me . . .' The ecstasy produced by this subjugation ritual was so great, V. E. confessed, that 'I literally thought would die.' The scenario is not regularly reenacted, she concludes: 'I don't think I could stand it.'

Richardson-style victims—innocents as hostages—have always played a large role in American life and American comics. They were, in fact, Richard Slotkin suggests in *Regeneration Through Violence*, among the earliest, the most necessary, and the most influential creations of the first seventeenth-century settlers: 'The basic factors in the physical and psychological situations of the colonists were the wildness of the land, . . . its unmitigated harshness . . . and the eternal presence of the native people of the woods, dark of skin and seemingly dark of mind, mysterious, bloody, cruel, "devil worshipping." To these must be added the sense of exile . . . the tearing up of home roots . . . exploration of new lands was one necessity . . .; fighting Indians, enduring captivity among them, and attempting to convert or enslave them were others. All emigrants . . . felt impelled to maintain traditions of religious order and social custom in the face of the psychological terrors of the wilderness . . . they could emphasize their English-ness by setting their civilization against Indian barbarism . . . in the accounts of the Indian Wars . . . the first American mythology took shape—a mythology in which the hero was the captive or the victim of devilish American savages. . . .'[5]

The twilit iconography of this mythology that was at one and the same time exculpatory and recriminative was illuminated in bright bold colors in the comic strips and comic books that adapted but preserved it essentially intact. In the comics as in the puritan accounts, innocence and simplicity are menaced by dark, exotic instruments of corruption and sophisticated duplicity. And as Richardson did, comic artists consistently objectified the endangered but enduring cultural values through such images as that of the virgin and adding, on their own, those of the naif, orphan, and lonely outsider. At one time or another and in one way or another, some of the best-known women in the best-known comics have consequently squirmed and cried through, and survived unviolated captivities and assaults almost identical to or designed to tease and tickle the same nerve ends set atremble by the struggles endured by Pamela.

As early as 1907 Charles Kahles, author of *Hairbreadth Harry*, was tying up his heroine, Belinda Blinks, and confronting her with the hideous dilemma of protecting her virtue and being sawn in half—longitudinally—or yielding to the lust of Rudolph Rassendale, a rank, musty, and unscrupulous villain who appeared always in top hat and tails and twirled his waxed mustache as he sneered down at his customarily fettered captive. For more than thirty-three years, Belinda was, with pious regularity on Sundays and often on weekdays, saved by her virtuous and asexual sweetheart, Harry. What such cartoonists as Kahles began was continued by scores of comic-strip artists and writers who followed him. Buck Rogers' Wilma, Flash Gordon's Dale, Dick Tracy's Tess, the Phantom's Diana, Mandrake's Narda, Popeye's Olive Oyl, Claude's Rosamond, Li'l Abner's Daisy Mae, Tarzan's Jane, Prince Valiant's Ilene, Joe Palooka's Anne Howe, Steve Canyon's Summer Olson (to cite only one of Milton Caniff's many maidens in distress), and Superman's Lois, along with many others, have separately but equally suffered countless close approaches to rape or some form of despoliation that sublimates it.

In a synopsis of a *Phantom* sequence that typifies the plot lines played out by Lee Falk, we read that 'deep in Bandar pygmy country an exhausted Lt. Byron is brought before the Phantom in the skull cave to deliver his tale of Diana in danger. Byron and Diana had barely survived the sinking of a freighter off the Bengal Coast. As they sat huddled around a fire with other survivors, a band of slave traders attacked, killing everyone except Byron and Diana. With Diana's assistance, Byron is able to slip away and bring help from the Phantom . . . Prince Ali drags Diana to Lord Suliman's oasis to make a sale.'[6] In the panels introduced by this synopsis, Diana escapes sexual servitude in Suliman's harem only because, fearing that her presence 'will bring soldiers,' Suliman orders Ali to bear her away. Ali, however, abandons her in the desert, where, he tells the readers, she is doomed: 'A day or so under the hot desert sun, without shelter, without food or water—and it's the end of her. That's enough! It's all over and forgotten.'[7]

Naturally, it is not all over. Eventually, 'the ghost who walks, the man who cannot die,' punishes Diana's tormentors and she is escorted to safety by Lt. Byron. Before her rescue, however, she wanders 'alone . . . somewhere on the vast, uncharted desert,' awakened at night by the 'eerie cries of jackals,' and tortured during the day by the 'pitiless broiling sun,' under which scorpions glitter in the sand—'sand—sand—sand—it's all sand everywhere.' Alex Raymond's 'The Outlaws of Mongo' adventure in *Flash Gordon* separates Dale from Flash and traps her in the subterranean retreat of Hong, 'evil lord of the dungeons' of Ming the Merciless. Hong, obese, Oriental, and, like Rudolph

Rassendale, wearing a waxed mustache (Hong's has tips that give it the look of a lethal weapon), inspects his new prisoners and sees Dale cringing in a bar-shadowed shaft of light in her otherwise pitch-black cell. 'Say, this is a pretty wench,' he hums malevolently as he peers at the cowering prisoner through heavily lidded eyes; 'Bring her to my office.' Desperately trying to fight off the mocking jailer who effortlessly clutches her wrists—'Come on, little one, you can't keep Hong waiting'—Dale is dragged to the dungeon Lord's office, where he at once pins her in his arms: 'I'll bargain with you little one—if you'll tell me where Flash is hiding, and become one of my wives, I won't disclose your identity to Ming.' Dale has no defense except a despairing shriek for help to Flash, who bursts in and disposes of Hong with his fists four or five panels later—too soon for Hong to do anything more damaging to Dale than to rip the shoulder of her blouse and expose the upper arc of her breast to his narrow-eyed inspection.[8]

Handsome, wholesome, ingenuous heroes are menaced by salacious sirens almost as often as the heroes' women are jeopardized by the too-keen appetites of the despicable debauchers whom *they* unyieldingly resist. Dale's Flash will serve as an example ready at hand. 'Into the Water World of Mongo,' one of the earliest ordeals to which Alex Raymond subjects his hero, throws Flash—literally—into the sea-bottom empire ruled by Queen Undina, whose first words to one of her guards as she sees Flash near death by drowning are, 'He is handsome—let him live, Triton—bring the lung machine.' His respiratory system adapted to breathing under water, Flash revives to hear Undina tell him, 'You're not drowned . . . but you'll have to live in the water world forever! You were too handsome to drown, so we changed your lungs . . .' 'But . . . no, you can't do that!' Flash protests, 'change me back quick!' 'Nothing can change you back,' Undina tells him, her arms folded resolutely beneath her ample breasts, her chin tilted upward and her eyes fixed levelly upon his: 'You are one of us forever.' Somewhat later, after warning Flash that 'You are my subject now,' she orders Pluton, a heavily muscled retainer, to teach Flash that 'I am supreme here . . . I want him to come crawling to me.'[9] Any readers who were unable to draw the correct implication from passages such as the preceding could turn, for explicit and graphic exegesis, to any one of the abundant erotic comics—variously referred to as 'Jo-Jo Books,' Tiajuana Bibles, or Eight Pagers—that, to borrow the terms of one of their few editors, 'flourished for a brief golden era in the 1930s.'[10]

As a central subject of several anonymously and wretchedly drawn specimens, Joe Palooka may be cited as a paradigm of his type. Cast as a guest at a cocktail party in one strip, Joe is gently but inescapably seized by a wanton whose opening remarks to him underscore his simplicity: 'Oh, I'm so sorry you can't drink, Joe . . .' Oafishly grateful to her for her unexpected attention, Joe thanks her and accepts her invitation to go with her to 'the library,' where, she adds meaningfully, 'we can be alone,' although Joe has just reminded her that 'Knobby says I gotta go to bed at 10 o'clock—you'se see, I'm in training.' The ploys used by the estrous and rutty Miss Van Loosbottom, as she is subsequently identified, are no more inventive or interesting than any of the others that quickly became stereotypes in comics of this warm and sticky sub-genre, but Joe's responses to them are, in the present context, well worth noting. Beads of sweat splash from his brow as she puts his hand on her breast and loosens his trousers. 'Oh no!' he gasps as she seeks to ensheathe him. His normal strength and vigor drained by shock and disbelief, Joe is unable to prevent her from throwing him upon his back and mounting him. Intimidated by her aggressiveness and blunt warning to 'cooperate or else,' he surrenders with resignation and becoming politeness: 'Well, if you'se insist, I must be a gentleman . . .'[11]

Joe, vulnerable because of his simple goodness and uncorrupted judgments, exemplifies not only those who suffer sexual danger in the comics but also that much larger group of amiable unfortunates who are victimized in various ways by circumstance, deceit, inhumanity, hypocrisy, cruel indifference, or their own susceptibility to misfortune.

Among the earliest of all such luckless or exploited figures was Frederick Burr Opper's 'Happy Hooligan,' whom Jerry Robinson has called, in his history entitled *The Comics*, 'A clownlike character with limitless good nature, the eternal fall guy . . . pathetic and ludicrous . . . the butt of his own good intentions that unfailingly backfired.'[12] From 1913 to 1944 *Krazy Kat* by George Herriman made an almost daily ritual of Ignatz's physical abuse of Krazy. Even though he believes that analysts should leave Krazy Kat alone, Robert Warshow in *The Immediate Experience* views Ignatz's inevitable attacks upon Krazy as a suggestion that 'evil always triumphs.'[13] The pessimism that Warshow somewhat reluctantly concedes might be found in Herriman's sequences can hardly be said to typify the prevailing attitude that the comics—until they went underground—have expressed toward life, deeds, and individual deserts. One could persuasively argue that, before the advent of the funky 'head comics' of the sixties, only Bud Fisher's *Mutt and Jeff* consistently shares with *Krazy Kat* a tendency to imply, by means of the ineptitudes and defeats that it chronicles, rueful contemplation of life's, and an innocent America's, hopes and purposes. From *Little Orphan Annie*, drawn by Harold Gray from 5 August 1924 until his death in 1968, to Charles Schulz's *Peanuts*, first seen in eight daily newspapers in October 1950, American comics have, of course, depicted good, upright, lovable creatures harried by persisting travail and mistreated by time, place, circumstance, and their fellows. Without their Chaplinesque difficult, ironic mishaps, and melodramatic afflictions, they wouldn't belong in the panels they dominate. But Annie and Charlie Brown—as well as Mickey Mouse, Popeye, Blondie and Dagwood, Li'l Abner, Pogo, Batman, Jiggs, Boob McNutt, and the Fantastic Four—reaffirm their, and our, capacity to endure. Like the elastic, flexible, indestructible characters of animated cartoons, Bugs Bunny or Wily Coyote, they are personifications of Life's resilience. The violence to which they are subjected is, as Jacob Brackman observed in 'The International Comix Conspiracy,' the 'old reversible sort of violence, where the puss who's been pancaked by a steam roller pops back into shape, or the rabbit who's just splattered to the ground from a thousand-foot cliff appears in the next panel wearing a Band-Aid.'

The underground or 'head' comics of the last decade seek no such accommodation with despair, no reaffirmation of the vitality of innocence. Distinguished from the traditional type in that they are often spelled *Comix* and appear, primarily, in stapled booklets, they specialize in a radically different treatment of the victims they present. Injury, debasement, rape, murder—provocatively potential in the old comics or reserved for monstrous, almost dehumanized evildoers—are commonplace disasters inflicted upon random sufferers in *Zap, Wonder Wart Hog, Rowlf, Fantagor, The Fabulous Furry Freak Brothers, Fritz the Cat, Inner City Romances, Girl Fight Comics,* and *Bizarre Sex.* 'Comics are never so naturalistic as when depicting mutilation or dismemberment,' Brackman wrote, calling attention to the link between sex and brutality in the work of such artists as Gilbert Shelton: '. . . sex and gore [are] inevitably conjoined. Genitals suddenly fall prey to angry maimings and castrations. (When a lady giggles at Wonder Wart Hog's wilted member, the hog of steel inserts his hideous snout instead and blows her all over the city.)'[14]

A ten-panel production entitled 'Heads or Tails' is a striking, if repellent, illustration of this conjunction of sex and gore. The spread opens with a wolf-like figure sitting on a small wharf at water's edge. He—or it—has a can of beer, a bamboo fishing rod with a heavy hook hanging from its end, and a bait can full of severed penises. 'Fine day for fishin'!' he says. In the panels that follow he baits his hook, which is immediately struck by a mermaid drawn by the prospect of irruption, violently jerks his catch onto the wharf, puts his foot on her back, chops her in half with a large cleaver, and walks off with a blood-spurting piece of tail. 'Fine day for fishin'!' he says, as a macabre antistrophic exit line.[15]

Some followers of underground comics have defended the seemingly demented and anarchic sadism thus displayed as a form of protest against the ritualized cruelties and hypocrisies legitimized by the unexamined conventions of the 'straight' world. 'Like any potentially subversive cultural mechanism,' Paul Buhle says in *Leviathan,* 'Komix serve . . . to destroy an old view of the old world and to replace it with a new one.'[16]

One writer close to Robert Crumb, author of *Mr. Natural, Fritz the Cat,* and other strips, cites a soliloquy of 'Whiteman,' 'the model that the middle-class dropouts of the Haight had . . . rejected,' as an example of Crumb's resort to violence and sexual fantasies as 'an attack on the "straight" culture's dictum that sex and anger are to be kept in tight rein at all costs': 'It's such an effort being polite to everyone. But if I stop, they'll see . . . they'll find out . . . my real self deep down inside . . . the raging lustful beast that craves only one thing, sex . . . I must maintain this rigid position or all is lost. Wow! This is hard work . . . I get headaches. My bowels refuse to function.'[17] Crumb himself has implied that the hardships and degradations he invents for his characters are perhaps his expression of rage and despair at what has happened to a sweet and tranquil America that still exists in his nostalgic idylls: 'As we get further and further away from that time, we are going to see that the twenties, thirties, and forties were the peak of American culture. It started declining after the thirties . . . in the twenties the popular level of the culture was really great. Nobody was especially conscious of it. It was just life. Did you ever look at an old photograph of a main street in an American town? They are really beautiful. Now those towns are dismal; everything is cheap plastic shit. If you come across an old small town that hasn't changed, it just makes you want to cry because it's so beautiful. Now you have to go to Disneyland to get that feeling.'[18]

No one even casually familiar with the figurative idiom traditional in American comics should be surprised that Crumb and his 'underground' compatriots articulate the despondent wrath behind comments of this type in a symbolic language that is predominantly sexual. Some, however, may be shocked by the ferocity, degradation, and diabolism that sound like ecstatically perverse dialectal corruptions of that standard tongue. S. Clay Wilson's 'Angels and Devils,' for example, begins with a slovenly angel, her extravagantly large breasts challenging the resources of her décolletage, responding to a drunken fellow-angel's command, 'thou shalt not take the name of the Lord thy God in vain.' 'No, no, no, no, never no never no never never never . . . I don't. No no no . . . You won't find me doin' that . . . no no no no no no Quack Blah blah blah nope quack.' Captions for the twenty-three panels that follow announce actions and situations such as these: 'A gaggle of devils . . . torturing a tart . . . timid martyrs . . . forced to suck the canes . . . of the devil's elders . . . the devils . . . disport themselves in unholy revelry [on] the sabbath . . . commit adultery . . . and steal . . . and bear false witness . . . covet . . . love themselves but despise all others.' Like most of Wilson's artwork, the illustration is almost a palimpsest of intricately combined forms and figures, a surrealistically intensified Brueghelian spread panoramically yet intimately representing an anthology of iniquities, sadistic cruelties, and depravities.[19]

Accompanying the gratuitous, explicit, and apparently sensational sexuality in the comix with an x is a distinctive tone that is alternatively broadly farcical, factitiously indignant, and ironically detached. Their brand of irony, much more, perhaps, than their obscenity, marks their difference from virtually all earlier examples of popular literature's use of sex. For their tensely unemotional attitude toward some of their most appalling inventions is matched by their authors' ruthlessly ironic view of themselves and the very work in which they express that ironic self-appraisal. On one of his back covers, Crumb tells his readers to 'take a tip . . . anyone can be a cartoonist. It's so simple a child can do it. Art is just a racket! A hoax . . .'[20] 'Got catholic guilt?' asks Justin Green at the end of his 'The Sage Monkey Debuts and Dies in "This Bitter Earth."'' 'Let me personally mail thee a copy of my informative yet entertaining comic: Binky Brown Meets The Holy Virgin Mary.'[21] The attitude here is that of a black humorist like Robert Coover, who pauses repeatedly in one of his stories, and abruptly abandoning the persona of the omniscient author, addresses his reader in whispered asides confessing skepticism concerning the same events about which he whispers to his reader: '. . . where is the caretaker's son? I don't know. He was here . . . Yet . . . there is no mention of the caretaker's son. This is awkward. Didn't I invent him myself . . . ? I don't know . . . to tell the truth, I sometimes wonder if it was not he who invented me . . .'[22]

The American colonists could resist and overcome the dark mysteries of the wilderness, Pamela could defend her chastity, and Belinda or Flash could reasonably rely upon benign coincidence, their own will, or the intercession of some guardian spirit to preserve their virtue undefiled. But what protects against experience, the species of 'knowing' that is one of the ambiguities intertwined in the old sexual metaphor? 'It is ironic,' Annie Dillard has said, 'that the one thing that all religions recognize as separating us from our creator—our . . . self-consciousness—is also the one thing that divides us from our fellow creatures. It was a bitter present from evolution, cutting us off at both ends.'[23] What the underground comics quite disturbingly do is seek to compel us to admit the incompatibility of the innocence we symbolically celebrate, sustain, or fear for in myth and the capacity for consciousness that is the glory and despair of *homo sapiens*, 'Knowing Man.'

Increasingly, furthermore, comics designed for a more general audience reveal introspective, introverted tendencies less self-destructive than but similar to the mocking sense of self abundantly in evidence in the 'undergrounders.' Captain America, with his affectedly appreciative comments on his own valor is an obvious instance. Less conveniently obvious but nevertheless pertinent are the situations upon which a series of recent syndicated strips is based. *Short Ribs* (begun in 1958) wryly juxtaposed the cowboys who were its central figures with anachronistic characters like cavemen and knights. A comparably calculating incongruity marks the association of Alfie and Sandy of *Dropouts* with aborigines of the island on which they are castaways. *Broom-Hilda* offers a witch who has ridden out of her historical past— her 'first husband was Attila the Hun, who owes her fifteen hundred years of back alimony . . .'[24] A reverse process operates in *Hagar the Horrible*: a twentieth-century idiom and framework of reference are transported into the protagonist's heroic Viking age. And *Doonesbury*, a successor of sorts to *Li'l Abner* and *Pogo*, is so sensible of its combination of what a news magazine identified a few months ago as its 'real and fictive' components,[25] that it is often as much a multi-paneled editorial-page cartoon as ordinary comic.

Our comics—strips and books, aboveground and underground— seem to be beckoning us away from the myths and legends of our own, and our nation's childhood. They are growing up, growing away, perhaps, from the heaven that Wordsworth believed 'lies about us in our infancy,' away from the romantic vision that 'man perceives . . . die away,/ and fade into the light of common day.' That's not very funny—is it?

☥ ☥ ☥ ☥ ☥

PARTICIPANT: *Do you regard the comics as an adult form rather than a children's form of literature?*

SAVAGE: Unfortunately, one of the problems of research in the comics is that many in the academic world regard the comics as distinctly children's literature and beneath the attention of the serious scholar. This is borne out by the fact that some of the very good collections held by universities are little used. This is not the case of European collections and a general attitude prevailing in the European research community. To come back to the question, I think the developments in comic books and later comic strips suggest they are getting more adult all the time. In fact, there is a close similarity between the development in comics and films and the kinds of comments I made about early comics applied very clearly to this film. You might consider comic strips as the first films, since they were 'shot' at the speed of four frames a day.

(Question on the attitude of Europeans toward those engaged in producing comics.)

SAVAGE: In Europe I think they are regarded more seriously as an art form than they are here. I have a friend, Steve Engelhardt, who draws—writes—Captain America. His complaint, always, is that he is generally regarded as an inconsequential writer of trivia here, but that in Europe, he is taken quite seriously.

NOTES

1. Samuel Richardson, *Pamela* (New York: W. W. Norton & Co., 1958), pp. 109, 116.

2. Ibid., pp. 212, 213.

3. Ian Watt, summarizing R. P. Utter and G. B. Needham, *Pamela's Daughters*, in *The Rise of the Novel* (Berkeley and Los Angeles: University of California Press, 1957), p. 161.

4. Ibid., p. 161.

5. Richard Slotkin, *Regeneration Through Violence: The Mythology of the American Frontier*, 1600–1860 (Middletown, Conn.: Wesleyan University Press, 1973), pp. 18, 21.

6. Bill Chadbourne, ed., *Nostalgia Comics*, issue no. 4 (New York: Nostalgia Press, 1973), p. 23.

7. Ibid., p. 24.

8. Alex Raymond, *Flash Gordon* (New York: Nostalgia Press, 1971), ch. 3, n.p.

9. Ibid., ch. 1, n.p.

10. J. M., ed., *A History of the Eight-Pagers: Dirty Comics* (Amsterdam, Holland: King Productions, n.d.), p. 5.

11. Ibid., pp. 112–13.

12. Jerry Robinson, *The Comics* (New York: Putnam's Sons, 1974), p. 30.

13. Quoted in Arthur Asa Berger, *The Comic-Stripped American* (New York: Walker Publishing Co., 1973), pp. 61, 63.

14. Jacob Brackman, 'The International Comix Conspiracy,' *Playboy* (December 1970), p. 328.

15. T. Boxell, 'Heads or Tails,' *Bizarre Sex*, 1:2 (November 1972), n.p.

16. Brackman, 'The International Comix Conspiracy,' p. 334.

17. Susan Goodrick, 'Robert Crumb,' *Apex Treasury of Underground Comics*, ed. Susan Goodrick and Don Donohue (New York: Links Books, 1974), pp. 13, 14.

18. Ibid., p. 15.

19. S. Clay Wilson, 'Angels and Devils,' *Zap Comics*, No. 6 (Apex Novelties, 1975), n.p.

20. Brackman, 'The International Comix Conspiracy,' p. 332.

21. Goodrick and Donohue, *Apex Treasury of Underground Comics*, p. 92.

22. Robert Coover, *Pricksongs and Descants* (New York: Dutton, 1970), p. 27.

23. Annie Dillard, *Pilgrim at Tinker's Creek* (New York: Harper's Magazine Press, 1975), p. 80.

24. Robinson, *The Comics*, p. 212.

25. 'Doonesbury: Drawing & Quartering for Fun & Profit,' *Time*, 107.6 (February 9, 1976):58.

II.
FILM ARCHIVES:
UNEXPLORED TERRITORY

MARSHALL DEUTELBAUM

While I did not originally choose the title for this talk, 'Film Archives: Unexplored Territory' provided me with both a clear focus and a happily cautionary note with which to organize these remarks. To be sure, the nature of a film archive—the way in which it differs from an audio-visual center, for example—has never puzzled those engaged directly in the study of the history and aesthetics of the motion picture. Yet with the growth in recent years of film study as an appropriate scholarly pursuit, many scholars in less obviously related disciplines have begun to inquire about the resources available to them in this nation's archives. Naturally, it is to this group that my comments are chiefly directed. And it is in this regard that I detect the need for a bit of caution.

I am reminded of the many fictitious maps offered the unwary tourist in Southern California which promise to reveal the locations of the movie stars' homes. In contrast to these bogus maps, I mean for my remarks to serve as an accurate and useful guide to the territory that a scholar can expect to encounter. Indeed the proper utilization of a film archive demands a clear understanding of archival goals. For this reason, I can suggest the scope of this paper in a series of questions: What is a film archive? What are an archive's goals? How best may a scholar make use of archival material? What limitations may a scholar expect to encounter in working in an archive?[1]

One might offer a deceptively simple definition of a film archive as a repository dedicated to the preservation of motion pictures. It is because of the word 'preservation' that this definition, though accurate, is more complicated than might otherwise appear to be the case. It is a dedication to the principle that a film in the possession of an archive will continue to be available to future generations in as close to its original form as possible. Since the life of a motion picture is finite, and diminishes with each projection, a film can only be made available for unlimited screening once an archive is certain that the continued existence of the film has been assured. Usually this takes the form of the preparation of a negative from which subsequent copies can be struck. No film is considered to be preserved, or protected for the future, unless such a negative has been prepared. Naturally, this requirement, the assurance of the continued accessibility of a specific film to future scholars, will sometimes limit the immediate availability of a film to a researcher.

The demands of preservation are even greater for motion pictures produced prior to 1950. From its inception in 1888, until about 1950, cellulose nitrate film stock was the mainstay for all 35mm theatrical motion pictures. Though this material provided a good base for photographic emulsions, and was supple enough to meet the physical demands of repeated projection, the cellulose nitrate base was inherently and unalterably unstable. As a first cousin to gun cotton, it has a low flash point and contains its own oxidant. Once ignited, it is virtually impossible to extinguish. Apart from the dangers it poses to those who must handle it, cellulose nitrate eventually becomes impossible to project due to shrinkage and decomposition. Though special storage vaults which keep temperature and humidity within specific limits can delay such decomposition for a while, the decay of cellulose nitrate stock cannot be halted.[2]

Only by copying these films onto cellulose triacetate film stock, 'safety acetate,' can the continued existence of all films made prior to 1950 be assured. The seriousness of the situation can be understood by reflecting upon the fact that less than 20 percent of the feature films produced in America during the 1920s still exist. To a large extent, the loss of the other 80 percent of the films produced during this period can be traced to the instability of the stock on which the photographic images were recorded. Naturally the preservation of cellulose nitrate films by transference to safety acetate stock is a major archival activity supported by funds from the federal government. Yet the job of copying these films is both costly and time-consuming, and much remains to be done. For this reason, many films which scholars might like to view will remain unavailable until transferred to safety acetate stock.

I realize that the limitations I have cited may seem severe, even in comparison to the restrictions imposed by rare manuscript collections. Yet I begin by citing these limitations in order to establish the context in which archival films may be used and to emphasize, as well, how fragile and precious these films are.

Turning to the film archives themselves, there are three major archival collections in the United States housed at the Library of Congress, the Museum of Modern Art, and at my own institution, the International Museum of Photography at George Eastman House in Rochester, New York. In addition, other sizable film collections are held by the University of California at Los Angeles Film Archives, the Pacific Film Archives in Berkeley, and the Wisconsin State Historical Society in Madison. Though each archive has its own unique flavor, the following remarks, drawn from the operation of Eastman House, accurately reflect the procedures one might expect to encounter, in general, when working with any of these institutions.

The International Museum of Photography at George Eastman House is dedicated to the preservation of the photographic image in all of its forms. Thus a large portion of the Museum's collection of still photographs, still negatives, and still photographic equipment falls outside the confines of my talk.[3] The Museum's Film Department maintains an archival collection of several thousand motion pictures, a collection of approximately three million motion picture still photographs, a large collection of motion picture cameras and associated apparatus, and a collection of books and periodicals related to motion pictures. All of the collections, which are steadily enlarged, are available for scholarly use by appointment. It is impossible to stress the need for an appointment too much. Demand for access to this archival material remains quite strong and it is common for our facilities to be booked up three months in advance. For this reason, it is wise for a scholar to contact an archive well in advance of the time when he would like to screen his films.

For a number of reasons, largely having to do with limitations of staff and facilities, no archive can arrange for immediate screenings. Films must be retrieved (no minor undertaking when a feature film can weigh eighty pounds), inspected to insure proper projection, then rewound and returned to the proper storage locations. Add the additional caution that must be used in projecting cellulose nitrate films, as well as time given over to the maintenance of projection equipment, and it is easy to see that the amount of time per week that is available for screening may often be severely limited. Naturally, the internal needs of each archive demand that some screening time be left open for the necessary use of the staff.[4]

Though these limitations are largely inflexible, another serious limitation is in the midst of being remedied. Apart from the Library of Congress, which maintains a card catalog listing the films in its collection that can be inspected at the Library, no other archive is yet able to offer a list of its holdings to prospective users. Both the Museum of Modern Art and Eastman House are preparing computer-generated catalogs which will be available upon demand. Unfortunately, it will be one to two years before these lists are generally available.[5] In the meantime, it remains necessary to inquire directly by mail about the availability of any specific title. Such letters are answered promptly and prove less of a hindrance than one might expect.

Limitations of screening space should underline the need for scholars to have already defined the area of their concern before they arrange for screenings. No archive can arrange more than a few days of screening for any individual at one time, and the desire to 'browse' through a number of films cannot be accommodated. Once again, screening time remains a precious commodity. Similar limitations exist on the amount of assistance that archival staff can offer to the researcher. While printed materials in archival collections are generally available for browsing, it is difficult for staff members to enter into lengthy research or correspondence regarding a scholar's particular area of interest.

Despite all of these limitations, there is a great deal of work that can and should be done. A specific description of the films in the Eastman House collection will suggest the array of available material. The Eastman House collection is especially rich in its holdings of silent American film, silent German Expressionist film, and in films produced during the Third Reich. Overall, the collection is representative and reflects the growth of the motion picture from its inception to the present time. Thus the early films of Edison, Lumière, and Melies exist together with the most recent works of Fellini, Bergman, and Antonioni. In this regard, the motion picture collection is a timeless time machine which allows the easy comparison of the past and present. For this reason, I might suggest some uses of the collection which could be made with regard to the role of children in these films.

Remarkably enough, the relationship between children and film antedates the invention of the movies. The earliest description of an optical toy based upon the persistence of vision—the physiological quirk which produces the illusion of motion—can be found in John Ayrton Paris's discussion of the Thaumatrope in *Philosophy in Sport Made Science in Earnest; Being an Attempt to Illustrate the First Principles of Natural Philosophy by the Aid of Popular Toys and Sports*, first published in London in 1827. (Eastman House holds both the three-volume first edition and a later one-volume American edition of Paris's delightful introduction to the natural sciences for children.) By the time of Edison's Kinetoscope and the first projected films of the 1890s, children were a staple of the domestic and comedy scenes that made up every program of films.

Though the fledgling film industry was quick to recognize the popularity of child actors, it was a great many years before the industry actually made an effort to produce films specifically intended for children.[6] Nevertheless, by 1910 most film companies had their own child stars who regularly appeared in films produced for general audiences. Curiously enough, despite the industry's inability to differentiate a specifically juvenile audience for its products, the films directed by D. W. Griffith at the Biograph studios between 1908 and 1912 illustrate how the development of cinematic technique could alter film narrative in regard to its subject matter.

Over the course of his time at Biograph, Griffith formed a stock company of juvenile performers. In part, his belief that a more natural acting style, rather than the theatrical mannerisms of the stage, was appropriate for motion pictures led him to select younger players not yet trained in such a histrionic style. In addition, Griffith's decision to photograph his players from closer range—mid-shot rather than long shot—also made the use of younger actors more desirable. The naturally superior muscle tone of these younger actors' faces, along with their lack of wrinkles, meant that they did not require the heavier make-up which would have been necessary for older performers and which the closer camera would have unavoidably recorded. Interestingly, his use of younger actors resulted in stories which were often presented from the point of view of someone their own age. Thus by using younger actors Griffith inadvertently produced films of interest to younger audiences, although it would be a mistake to call any of them children's films in the current sense.

It is difficult to determine precisely when the industry chose to produce films specifically designed for children. To be sure, problems of censorship, or of threatened censorship, which resulted from children viewing films intended for adults, perpetually kept the industry aware of this group as a potential audience. By the mid-teens many exhibitors had experimented with matinees in an attempt to offer an alternative to evening fare for children. These experiments, however, were fitful and unsuccessful. The problem is described in a 26 August 1916 article entitled 'Motion Pictures for Children: Country Wide Movement by Prominent Women— What Has Been Accomplished and What is Being Attempted,' appearing in *The Moving Picture World*, one of the major trade periodicals of the time.

Noting the general failure of previous programs attempting to attract children, the writer cites the following factors:

> The scarcity of film, which is at the same time thrilling and considered suitable by particular people for young minds, the lack of interest on the part of parents, or of co-operation on the part of exhibitors, or often the presentation of programs of pictures which are too educational to attract and hold children who have grown accustomed to the usual theater program, have been accountable for failure in many places.[7]

As these comments suggest, the drive for programs suitable for children was strongly motivated by a sense of moral purpose. This is especially clear in the case of children's films presented in Providence, Rhode Island. Organized by a Mrs. Dexter Thurber, who was assisted by a professor from Brown University, this series appears to have placed a greater emphasis on the decorum of its juvenile audience than upon the films themselves:

> 'From the first we have tried to make children's performances "the thing",' says Mrs. Thurber, 'and for that reason we have been most careful to keep everything strictly first class. We found that every child responded to the environment—even the children who had been accustomed to attending the cheapest and most luridly advertised theater were quiet and orderly even in their applause. It is the object of the people who are most active in the movement for children's programs in Providence to educate children up to proper behavior in public places as well as to appreciate real artistic films.'[8]

The sense of moral uplift which apparently motivated most of these children's programs is evident in the remarks concerning a series presented in Boston which was organized by Mrs. Edith Dunham Foster, of the Community Motion Picture Bureau. Drawing upon her experience as a writer, editor, and social worker,

> Mrs. Foster carefully selects pictures which she knows will satisfy the demand of the types of audiences she is supplying with programs. For the sophisticated children, and for a performance offered to rival the lurid and sensational drama of the poorer houses, she picks out thrillers of the western pioneer and Indian type, baseball, comedy and anything that contains clean, legitimate action. For the children who have not become movie fans she arranges programs of fairy tales, animal and nature studies, scenics and lighter dramas and comedies.[9]

It is interesting to find the children divided into two groups: one already familiar with movies for whom less objectionable fare is provided; the other not yet devoted to films (perhaps not having been permitted to attend movies) for whom much lighter subjects are provided.

By the late teens, the larger Hollywood studios were producing films specifically designed for children, and it would be worth-while to determine how much effect the work of these women's organizations had upon the decision to produce such films. To my knowledge, no one has undertaken such a study. Considering the general development of film history at this period, the interest of upper-class and upper-middle-class women in the presentation of films suitable for their own children parallels the growing acceptance of films as legitimate entertainment for adults by these same social groups.[10] For this reason alone, research into the development of films for children during this period should yield fruitful results.

(*Viewing of film, 'The Cry of the Children.'*)

ᵀ ᵀ ᵀ ᵀ ᵀ

PARTICIPANT: *Are you preparing 16mm prints rather than 35mm projection prints from 35mm negatives?*

DEUTELBAUM: Yes, more and more. These 16mm prints are reference prints. In other words, we can show them to people; we can wear them out; we can loan them. We can allow people to run them in the museum. Happily enough they are a coincidental by-product of making a 35mm acetate negative from 35mm nitrate originals. Our primary interest is image quality: what the image looks like on the screen. When we make a 35mm acetate negative, for preservation purposes, there is no way to tell how good the negative is unless we make a positive as well. So, what we often do is make a 35mm acetate negative from 35mm nitrate materials and then make what we call a test print, which is 16mm, to judge the quality of the negative copy. Increasingly we are building up duplicate prints on 16mm for reference use. We are also trying to print up films that are in greater demand in 16mm as well.

(*Question from audience having to do with the projection of films and projection speed.*)

DEUTELBAUM: During the silent period, up until sound came in, at which time projection speed was standardized at a constant twenty-four frames a second, all the films were photographed by hand-cranked cameras. Directors would vary the speed at which the camera was cranked for emotional effect. Sometimes they would undercrank it, which means the action would appear to take place faster. Sometimes they would crank it very fast, which would slow it down. Such changes of tempo could occur many times within the same film. It is hard to reproduce this unless you have a rheostat on the projector. Even then, it is difficult to know precisely how it was shown originally, and I think this print of 'The Cry of the Children' is typical of what you run into. I think it looks very good at twenty-four frames a second. We showed it at sound film speed. Common, though mistaken, popular wisdom holds that any film from 1912 ought to be shown now at what most 16mm projectors label as 'silent speed.' This is a speed of eighteen frames per second. In other words, this rate of projection would have added 25 percent to the running time of 'The Cry of the Children.' You saw it as a twenty-minute film. It would have run twenty-five to twenty-six minutes if run at 'silent speed.' The actions would have taken forever, and I think the movement here for most of the film looked pretty good. While there are other films from this period which would still look too fast if projected at even eighteen frames per second, arriving at what might be a proper speed remains difficult. The only compensation is that once one has had a chance to see a number of silent films, one adapts to varying rates of speed and internalizes them. It doesn't get in the way.

(Question about distribution of 'The Cry of the Children' and where it was photographed.)

DEUTELBAUM: The distribution on this would have been fairly good. The Tannhauser Company films were well distributed. At the time the child labor laws were enacted, the film was described and read into the Congressional Record as part of the debate. It was well-known and well-advertised in a number of ways. Unfortunately, all the records of the company are lost, and we have not been able to determine who directed it, or where that mill is—if that is a real mill, or where that shanty is, if it is a real one—somewhere around New Rochelle, I suspect, but we are not sure.

PARTICIPANT: *How typical is this film in reflecting a socially activist point of view?*

DEUTELBAUM: It's pretty much in the mainstream of American films going back to 1905/6. I'm thinking of an Edison film of 1906 called 'The Kleptomaniac,' which turns on a wealthy woman who is a shoplifter, and how justice for the wealthy is much softer than justice for a poor woman who steals a loaf of bread to feed her children. Griffith in 1909 deals with temperance in a film titled 'The Drunkard's Reformation.' In it, it is the child who brings her father to reform his drinking habits. Social concerns run through a great many films of the early years—especially those produced by Edison and Biograph.

NOTES

1. A useful bibliography of articles dealing with film archives can be found in Richard Dyer MacCann and Edward S. Perry, eds., *The New Film Index: A Bibliography of Magazine Articles in English,* 1930–1970 (New York: Dutton, 1975), pp. 19–20. In addition, descriptions and addresses of all the world's archives are provided in Peter Cowie, ed., *International Film Guide 1976* (New York: A. S. Barnes, 1975). The list is updated in each annual volume.

2. The current technology regarding the preservation of cellulose nitrate film, along with the problems associated with the preservation of color film stock and magnetic recordings, is summarized in Ralph N. Sargent and Glen Fleck, eds., *Preserving the Moving Image* (Washington, D.C.: The National Endowment for the Arts and the Corporation for Public Broadcasting, 1974).

3. For a discussion of the still photographic holdings of the International Museum of Photography at George Eastman House see Robert A. Sobieszek, 'The International Museum of Photography at George Eastman House: The Research Center: A Brief Introduction,' *The University of Rochester Library Bulletin,* 28 (Winter 1975): 109–122.

4. For a lengthy discussion of the ways in which similar limitations may restrict access

to the Film Study Center of the Museum of Modern Art see Charles Silver, 'Using MOMA,' *American Film*, 1(May 1976):72–3.

5. Currently in preparation, the *Union Catalogue of Motion Picture and Television Manuscript and Special Collections*, when completed, will provide a guide to film-related holdings on the West Coast. For further information on this project see Linda Harris Mehr, 'Union Catalogue to be Unique Resource,' *The Magazine*, 'Special Issue' (November/December 1975). Published by The Film and Television Study Center in Los Angeles, *The Magazine* may well prove a useful guide to film collections in the area.

6. For the details of one early attempt see Kevin Brownlow, 'The Franklin Kid Pictures,' *Films in Review* 23(August/September 1972):396–404.

7. Betty Shannon, 'Motion Pictures for Children: Country-Wide Movement by Prominent Women—What has been Accomplished and What is Being Attempted,' *The Moving Picture World* 29(August 26, 1916):1407.

8. Ibid., 1408.

9. Ibid.

10. The significance of children's film programs in upper-class neighborhoods is suggested in 'Children's Matinee Idea Grows,' *The Moving Picture World* 29(August 26, 1916):1435.

12.
SUMMARY AND COMMENTARY

FRANCES HENNE

The only fair and accurate way to summarize the content of the papers presented in this Symposium would be to hand each of you copies of the papers. These papers have been crammed with interesting and illuminating material reporting findings of research, techniques of inquiry and searching, available and needed resources, and other data.

Without going into findings, I can only repeat and note some obvious factors for those papers related to social history in children's literature and in illustrations. In overall nature and design, the papers dealt with a variety of topics and formats within a wide range of contexts. We have heard the results of studies made in the realms of art history, social history, social geography, cultural history, and literary history—a composite of interdisciplinary research. The methodologies used covered a variety of approaches (picture, theme, subject, language, and character analyses, among them). Philosophical and theoretical concepts shaping the theory of the study and analysis of children's literature were incorporated in some of the papers.

Several conclusions reached in some of the research papers supported the findings, in terms of trends, attitudes, and emphases, in other research papers at this Symposium. Those presenting these papers, you recall, commented on these similarities and relationships which could be found even though the studies had different focuses and covered different time periods. Also, when a study was concerned with a longer time span, some characteristics of the literature were similar for the different periods covered. Some recurrent observations related to fiction can be sketchily summarized in the following listing:

An emphasis on moral education characterizes the nineteenth-century publications. (We have our own twentieth-century equivalent in many currently published children's books!) From early times, behavior and consequences, an inseparable pair and a recurring motif, depict the dire results of inappropriate behavior, frequently with violence portrayed in text and illustrations.

Fiction is an agent of socialization. Several social themes and

183

values appear again and again. There is an emphasis on non-urban values.

Books and stories speak of their time, even though not of their events precisely. Nationalism is represented in principles rather than in events.

The authors are respectful of children who are 'taken seriously as moral beings.'

Certain story patterns emerge (one speaker presented two fiction formulas), and requisites exist that define regionalism in fiction. Evolutionary developments can be observed in regional literature and also in the literature relating to moral and social behavior. Some ideas persist, although their treatment may adapt and change.

There is a notable absence of literary quality.

The characteristics, values, and purposes of the authors become evident in their writings (many authors represented the cultural elite and the cultural gentry).

All in all, a relationship exists between culture and society and literature for children. Social historical research in the area of children's literature contributes to an understanding not only of the past but also of the present.

A few cautionary comments should be made about some of the hazards of research. Some of these have been mentioned by those presenting papers and by participants in the audience. Four major types can be noted:

In many ways we are dealing with adult values rather than with children's values. The books that we examine do not necessarily reflect children's likes or preferences. We must always recognize the role of adults in creating these materials and making them accessible during any given period. We must be aware, too, of the role of adults in interpreting the content and status of these materials in later times. The possibility lurks of interpreting other times in terms of our own contemporary conditions or atmosphere. Hence we often consider books to be quaint, amusing (when they are far from amusing), or dreary and dull, when in reality they might not have been so considered by the children.

We are dealing only with what is available or accessible during the time period studied, and can determine very little about effects or even how much was read, viewed, or listened to by any known number of individuals. Studying just what is published or produced in a particular period may be limited in several ways if we ignore what would still be accessible although published/ produced prior to that time. Obviously, the unavailability of materials (including ones of quite recent vintage) frequently creates a handicap for the scholar.

Related to the two preceding observations would be that of noting that we cannot ignore the presence and the reading of adult works by children — adult works in the original and not just those adapted for youth.

Finally, we cannot categorically reject the belief of some critics that a time lag occurs between the presence of adult concerns in society and the appearance of these concerns in books for children. Other critics have commented on the time lag taking place before literary styles and themes found in adult books appear in children's books.

The second part of the Symposium was concerned with the resources of research. Many kinds of resources were mentioned: children's books and periodicals, illustrations in children's books; comic strips, films, and other types of materials; public and research libraries, libraries in publishing houses and in cultural centers of ethnic groups, and private collections; manuscripts, original art, and correspondence of authors and artists; correspondence and other material of publishers; and bibliographic and reference works. Specific recommendations for descriptive bibliographies, information tools, and compendia needed to facilitate the research of scholars were made for different areas, periods, and locales of children's literature; these studies in themselves constitute an important branch of research.

Cost data for the preservation of materials in research libraries were presented, as were descriptions of various techniques employed in the physical preservation of materials. Microfilming as a means for building collections was noted as a trend. Although time did not permit discussion in detail, the importance of planning among librarians and others emerged as a key factor in assuring coverage and preservation of resources, in eliminating pointless competition, and in establishing an apparatus of bibliographic control that would facilitate research and other uses of resources. It is to be hoped that such planning might also provide a solution to a current problem revolving around the difficulties encountered in getting research published—significant research that may have a limited audience or that may entail considerable expenditure for the reproduction of illustrations or other content.

Not knowing what resources are available and not being able to find materials were described as conditions creating handicaps for those doing research and limiting research in general. One speaker noted that available resources can open up research that would not otherwise be undertaken.

A plea was made that more library schools offer courses dealing with descriptive and systematic bibliography of a scholarly nature and with the preservation of materials. For each area, the number of courses now available is scant indeed.

From all of these discussions, we can obtain guides and suggestions of what scholars might want and need for their research: the literature itself in all its formats and materials relating to it. Start collecting today!

A third and integral part of this Symposium has been your participation in the discussion periods. An analysis of your questions and what they represent—not the content of answers to your questions—opens up other avenues for inquiry and further deliberations. Some topics seemed to recur: the relationships and differences between American and British literature for children; the patterns of children's reading of materials falling outside the scope of the papers—fables, folklore, adult popular fiction, and others; the nature, if any, of American fantasy; facts relating to publishers, printers, and distributors of books during different time periods; and the stereotyping of minorities, immigrants, rural workers, and other groups.

With the research and other work that has already been done and is underway and with the contribution of this Symposium, we move steadily toward the position where we can construct a vast panorama that clearly identifies children's literature in society and society in children's literature. This panorama would be arranged in parallel columns or 'streams' so that interrelationships between and among the various columns and their contents could be observed for different periods of time in the United States. One column would be devoted to each of the areas listed below and the content for each. One column would be arranged in chronological order:

1. Major socioeconomic characteristics and social conditions for the various classes of society.

2. The status, characteristics, and activities of children in society (including adult attitudes toward children); the role of the family; leisure-time activities; and related factors.

3. The education of youth: curricular content, instructional methods (including the objectives and methods of teaching reading, viewing, and listening); legislation pertaining to education; characteristics of the school population.

4. The moral, ethical, and religious climate.

5. The humanistic scene, both traditional and innovative: art (adult) and art by and for children; music, both classical and popular; the literary scene for children and adults; attitudes of adults toward quality, purposes, and characteristics of children's literature; aspects of popular culture and 'taste.'

6. Communications: status of reading, viewing, and listening; literacy, illiteracy, and functional illiteracy patterns; channels; use.

7. Publishing and production of materials for children in the United States; creators of literature for children.

8. Highlights in the publishing/production of children's literature in other countries.

9. Types, format, and content of children's literature (all media formats and all types of materials within those formats).

10. The reading, viewing, and listening patterns and interests of children.

11. Accessibility of materials for children: in libraries for children, in college and university libraries, in bookstores, homes, and other outlets; policies affecting the accessibility of materials.

12. Landmark events in the world.

Our thanks go to the School of Library Science of Simmons College, to the Children's Services Division of the American Library Association and its Committee on National Planning for Special Collections, and to the Planning Committee and Cooperating Organizations of the Symposium for designing and presenting this conference; to our speakers for their interesting and illuminating papers; and to you, the participants, for coming from all parts of this country and from Canada, for giving evidence of your interest in and enthusiasm for social history and children's literature, and for your penetrating observations and questions. Now, each of you has been imbued anew or for the first time with the desire of doing some research (no matter how modest the scale, it is important) and of becoming a personal collector of some type of children's literature, particularly, perhaps, materials of recent vintage that will be difficult to find a few years hence. The Symposium has given further impetus and support to your professional activities, wherein research is encouraged and implemented and the resources of research are preserved and made accessible.

The literature for children of a country does indeed reflect the mores, characteristics, concerns, values, and goals of that country, and represents a very real, very vital bloodstream in the cultural and social life of a nation.

APPENDIX I
Genesis of a Research Collection

First of all I want to say how pleased we all are to have the Symposium participants visit the Boston Public Library and pleased to cooperate once again with the Simmons Library School in promoting programs of mutual interest and concern. The Boston Public Library is vitally interested and concerned in the topic occupying this symposium. The importance of children's literature needs no elucidation with this group. One of my concerns as an administrator has been in building upon the great strength of this library and its historical interest in children's work. Now perhaps you ought to be listening to Ruth Hayes, our distinguished emeritus coordinator of children's services, rather than me; but I think perhaps the only reason you are here to listen to me is for encouragement. I hope the directors of our other large research libraries will maintain or generate an interest in children's literature.

Two years ago with the cooperation of members of our library staff, but most particularly Priscilla Moulton, with the expert advice of Jim Fraser, and the help of Ann Pellowski and others, we decided to do something about the international aspect of children's literature which goes along with our concern for developing a concerted program of historical collecting in the area of children's literature. Library administrators must realize the importance of children's literature—not only recognize but actively support programs for the development of historical collections as well as services. But I should qualify my comments by saying that the term historical collections does not refer just to the early children's books. For this area in large measure we can leave to Fred Bauer and his associates at the American Antiquarian Society, an institution which has developed a tremendous collection of early American children's books. Certainly we are very happy to acquire early children's books in the field that is the special responsibility of the American Antiquarian Society, but we are not out to compete with them in acquiring any titles which come upon the market. I think it is important in this area, as in all other areas, to realize that tomorrow's history is today's acquisition. And it is from this standpoint that this library started its development in a concerted way—a program which has been underway for the last seventy-five years here in the Boston Public Library. The Library has collected books relating to children's literature, used these books, has worn them out, has acquired some illustrations which have gone into our print department, but it has not segregated and identified as a separate collection children's literature materials.

So three years ago we decided we were going to embark on a program, pulling together the materials which existed not only in the children's room. We withdrew some material from branches and acquired collections from other libraries which no longer had any real interest or concern for maintaining children's books outdated from a service standpoint. We are currently withdrawing books from our stack collection and are putting these together in what we are calling our 'historical collection.' This collection has been named in honor of Alice M. Jordan, who was in a sense the founder of children's work here in the Boston Public Library. Through this collection, we have been very fortunate to have been able to acquire the collection of Ruth Hill Viguers, a distinguished leader in children's literature. We also decided to develop a tripartite program of collecting children's literature: selecting materials for active use in our children's library for borrowing purposes in our central library and in our library branches; forming a collection of books which have been identified by our children's specialist as important books for the training of children's librarians, for the use of authors and illustrators, parents and other groups; and developing the Jordan collection. To this collection we have been adding one copy of each children's book which we acquire yearly. This means that we have been systematically adding a significant representation of quality children's books published in this country. At least this is our goal.

A few years ago we decided this was to be a collection of not only books published in the United States, but one which would reflect this publishing phenomenon worldwide. In order to do this, we came up with the concept of 'Children's Books International,' an annual exhibition and programs of a month's duration centering on various global publishing efforts. Our reasons were twofold: First, we wanted to make available current books for children from various parts of the world for the different language groups which go into making up our metropolitan community. Secondly, we wished to do a thorough job of collecting for research purposes. From my own experience in the academic field on an international level, it has been my observation that this was one major area of neglect among research libraries.

So, with this in mind, we have added foreign and domestic children's literature to our collecting program at the Boston Public Library. We have arrangements with major dealers in all countries in Western Europe, all countries in Latin America, a number of countries in Eastern Europe, the Soviet Union and elsewhere, a children's component to the blanket order of arrangements which we have with more than sixty countries around the world. In addition to that which we are selecting on an individual basis, we are monitoring the materials which are supplied to the library. We have our dealers send us checked copies of the bibliographies. That will indicate what they are sending, and our staff has a responsibility of evaluating these, refining the collecting programs where necessary, and expanding the collections where necessary. It is not enough just to acquire these books; we want to have them used, not only in the central library, but in our branch libraries. We also feel a responsibility for a long-range development of the collection of materials from the various parts of the world. I think this is an area where libraries have the opportunity to make significant contributions to world understanding, an opportunity that no other segment of society can provide, and if we pursue this on a broad enough scale, I think that slowly but surely, we can have an impact on advancing world peace and understanding. Now, in order to highlight our aims and goals, we decided to establish an annual program—'Children's Books International,' working with Combined Books USA. Publishers' representatives from various countries were contacted and requested to supply books of current interest. We realize that this is not a library selective process; but I believe we need to look at the materials that the youngsters are actually reading, and we know that much of this literature does not meet even our minimum standards of acceptance. Still, these books are important in themselves and are certainly of research value. I look at the antiquarian book market and see some of the prices of the books which librarians of fifty or even fifteen years ago would not allow in their building; but these were the books the youngsters were reading. Today we are collecting them because of their historical interest; because of their reflection of the society of the day. I think this is a responsibility of the library. As for use by children, I am not saying we should have these books necessarily for all youngsters to read; I'm not saying we shouldn't have them. This is a question which I will leave to those of you who specialize in making such judgments. From an historical perspective, these materials are important because if one is going to have an understanding of the social life of a time, one has to have the bad as well as the good. I can recall in the adult field several years ago spending time and money trying to put together for Howard Mumford Jones a collection of the second-, third-, and fourth-rate American fiction for the course he was giving in American literature. I can also recall a decision that was made when *Sports Illustrated* was first published that the Harvard Library would not subscribe to it. A few years later we were looking for a back file of *Sports Illustrated* in regard to its social and educational importance, and I think we face a similar situation in the field of children's literature.

But that is getting away from my point and the international aspect. We decided to arrange this annual conference on 'Children's Books International,' bringing together books for all to see, but also highlighting this with experts from various parts of the world, so that we could expose the library community to these experts and see what they had to offer. In our first year we had talks by Carla Poesio (Italy), Leny Dornelles (Brazil), Kazue Mizumura (United States), Mollie Hunter (Scotland), as well as speakers from the United States. This year we had a varied and interesting program and offered a French translator, Edward Fenton, who gave a magnificent talk. Once it is published, I think it will be regarded as a classic comment on translation, not only on how it affects children's literature. I think it is one of the best lectures I have ever heard given on the subject, and I believe will be required reading in children's-literature courses in library schools. I would suggest it should be read by every librarian interested in the area of translation.

We did concentrate on animated film, but we introduced also an adult component into this since we were dealing to some extent with folktales and folk ways, which are an important part of children's literature. We invited Albert Lord, the distinguished professor at Harvard, to speak on the eclectic process in the development of folk literature, folk poetry from the Balkans, and William Ready of the McMaster University Library in Canada, who spoke on Welsh tales. I think it is important for us to indicate the nexus between folklore, the folktale, the folkpoem, the folk-song on the adult level—the entire history and then its evolution into literature for children. Then, we were most fortunate to have Duŝan Roll, a worldwide expert on graphics in the children's literature field. We don't know what next year will bring, but we are thinking in terms of contemporary illustration because particularly with children the role of graphics is vitally important.

Now, aside from the research aspect, I think all of this is indicative of the fact that this library is concerned about its identification with children's literature, for supplying children's literature to the youngsters in the Boston metropolitan and the statewide level—literature which the youngsters will read and enjoy. We will supply this in their native language, if they are recent immigrants, or we will try to encourage them to have an interest in and concern for their heritage. I think that we have seen throughout the history of this country the first and second generation of people completely ignoring the heritage of their parents. By the third generation, you find them coming back and specializing in the field of culture relating to their background as they go on to college. The losses to us and to the generations' neglect of their heritage are difficult to measure. We hope that by emphasizing where appropriate the children's literature in various languages, we will make a contribution in keeping alive a cultural interest in the first generation while trying to awaken an interest in second and third generations. Further, we must take the opportunity that we have through children's literature and libraries to make other groups aware of the contributions of the individual ethnic groups.

This is the program we have embarked on, and we are making available a great deal of staff time and money to this end. I hope by the end of this decade we will have made a significant contribution toward these concepts which I have outlined. The collection now totals, I believe, sixty to seventy thousand volumes, and by concentrating on the present so that we won't have gaps that will have to be filled in the future, we can then go back and fill in gaps either by individual purchase or by special collections, which is even better.

This is the program of the Boston Public Library. We hope it is encouraging to all people working in the field of children's literature to see the rapid growth over the last several years. Again, I am glad you were able to come to the Library. I have talked longer than I intended, but it is an area in which I am vitally interested.

—*Philip J. McNiff*

APPENDIX 2

Symposium Program

9:00   Registration

9:30   Opening Statement on *American society as reflected in children's literature*
Frances Henne, Ph.D., Professor Emerita and Special Lecturer in Library Services, School of Library Service, Columbia University

10:00   *Children's literature and American culture, 1820–1860*
Anne Scott MacLeod, Ph.D., Assistant Professor, College of Library and Information Service, University of Maryland

11:15   Break

11:30   *Social factors shaping some late nineteenth-century children's periodical fiction*
R. Gordon Kelly, Ph.D., Assistant Professor, Department of American Civilization, University of Pennsylvania

12:30–1:30   Luncheon—The Press Room

2:00   *Regionalism in the American children's book*
Fred Erisman, Ph.D., Associate Professor, Department of English, Texas Christian University, and Editor of *American Literary Realism*

3:15   Break

3:30   *The foreign language press and children's literature in the United States*
James H. Fraser, Ph.D., Director, Friendship Library, Fairleigh Dickinson University, and Editor of *Phaedrus*

4:00   *Children's book illustrations in the documentation of American social life*
Edgar deN. Mayhew, Ph.D., Director, Lyman Allyn Museum, and Professor of Art History, Connecticut College
Jane C. Nylander, Curator of Textiles and Ceramics, Old Sturbridge Village

5:00–6:00   Exhibition of Children's Books International, Boston Public Library

Genesis of a research collection
Philip J. McNiff, Director and Librarian, Boston Public Library

Reception—Boston Public Library

MAY 15   THE RESOURCES FOR RESEARCH

9:00   *Eighteenth-century children's books: the economics, preservation, and bibliographic control*
Frederick E. Bauer, Jr., Associate Librarian, American Antiquarian Society
Gerald Gottlieb, Curator of Early Children's Books, Pierpont Morgan Library
Howell J. Heaney, Librarian, Rare Book Department, Free Library of Philadelphia

10:30   Coffee

10:45   *Manuscripts, original art and creators of children's books*

Marjorie G. Wynne, Research Librarian, Beinecke Rare Book and Manuscript Library, Yale University

11:30 *Researching the American children's picture book*
Barbara Bader, Editor, Kirkus Reviews

12:15–1:15 Luncheon—The Press Room

1:30 *Lost innocence in the American comic strip*
Walter Savage, Ph.D., Professor, Department of English, Fairleigh Dickinson University

2:30 *Film archives: unexplored territory*
Marshall Deutelbaum, Assistant Director Film Department, International Museum of Photography at George Eastman House

3:15 Summary by Frances Henne, Ph.D.

4:00 Adjournment

PLANNING COMMITTEE

James H. Fraser
Chairman, Committee on National Planning for Special Collections, American Library Association

Margaret Mary Kimmel
Assistant Professor, School of Library Science, Simmons College

Priscilla Moulton
Director of Library Services, Public Schools, Brookline, Massachusetts

Robert D. Stueart
Dean and Professor, School of Library Science, Simmons College

Timothy W. Sineath
Assistant Professor and Arrangements Coordinator, School of
Library Science, Simmons College

COOPERATING ORGANIZATIONS

American Antiquarian Society
195 Salisbury Street, Worcester, Massachusetts 01609

Boston Athenaeum
10 ½ Beacon Street, Boston, Massachusetts 02108

Boston Public Library
P.O. Box 286, Copley Square, Boston, Massachusetts 02117

The Congregational Library
Congregational House, 14 Beacon Street, Boston, Massachusetts
02108

David R. Godine, Publisher
306 Dartmouth Street, Boston, Massachusetts 02116

Goodspeed's Bookshop, Inc.
18 Beacon Street, Boston, Massachusetts 02108

Horn Book, Inc.
585 Boylston Street, Boston, Massachusetts 02116

Phaedrus, Inc.
14 Beacon Street, Boston, Massachusetts 02108

CONTRIBUTORS

Frederick E. Bauer, Jr.
Associate Librarian, American Antiquarian Society

Marshall Deutelbaum
Assistant Director Film Department, International Museum of Photography at George Eastman House

Fred Erisman
Associate Professor, Department of English, Texas Christian University, and Editor of *American Literary Realism*

James Fraser
Director of Friendship Library, Fairleigh Dickinson University, Editor of *Phaedrus*, and Chairman of the Committee on National Planning of Special Collections, Children's Services Division, American Library Association

Gerald Gottlieb
Curator of Early Children's Books, Pierpont Morgan Library

Howell J. Heaney
Librarian, Rare Book Department, Free Library of Philadelphia

Frances Henne
Professor Emerita and Special Lecturer in Library Services, School of Library Service, Columbia University

R. Gordon Kelly
Assistant Professor, Department of American Civilization, University of Pennsylvania

Anne Scott MacLeod
Assistant Professor, College of Library and Information Service, University of Maryland

Walter Savage
Professor, Department of English, Fairleigh Dickinson University

Marjorie G. Wynne
Research Librarian, Beinecke Rare Book and Manuscript Library, Yale University

INDEX

Abner, Li'l, 156, 159
Abolition. See Fiction, children's, anti-slavery sentiment in.
Abramowicz, Dina, 83, 84
Adam, R. B., 140
Adams, Maude, 147
Adventure, Mystery and Romance (Cawelti), 35
Aesop, 131, 147
Aikin, John, *Letters from a Father to His Son*, 100
Alcott, Louisa M., 41, 46
Aldrich, Thomas B., *Story of a Bad Boy*, 16, 47, 56, 58–9
Alger, Horatio, 29, 46
America, image of, 161
American Antiquarian Society, 96, 102, 106, 189
American Children's Books, 1723–1939 Catalogue Six. (Edward Morrill & Son), 99
American Institute for Conservation, 116
American Picturebooks from Noah's Ark to the Beast Within (Bader), ix
American Psychological Association, viii
American Revolution, 18, 20
American Sunday School Union, 26
'Angels and Devils' (Wilson), 161
Antiquarian book market, inflation, 99, 101
Antonioni, Michelangelo, 172
Arbeitskreis für Jugendliteratur, vii
Archives, motion picture, 169, 171–2, 178
Armenian children's literature, 82–3, 90–1
Armenian General Benevolent Union, 83
Armenian Language Laboratory (New York City), 91
Armenian National Library (Erevan), 91
Arnold, Matthew, 143
Ash, Lee, *Subject Collections*, 80
Asimov, Isaac, 72
Asquith, Cynthia, 146
At the Back of the North Wind (MacDonald), 141
Auctions, book, 98–101

Bader, Barbara, ix
Banks, Paul, 112
Barahura, Walter, 89
Barbauld, Mrs., 129, 139

Barbier, A. A., *Dictionnaire des ouvrages anonymes*, 130
Barrie, J. M., 146–7, 149
The Bartholomew-Tide Fairing, 124
Batman, 159
Bauer, Fred, 189
Baum, L. Frank, 59, 65; *The Wonderful Wizard of Oz*, 58
Baylor, Frances C., *Juan and Juanita*, 58
Bayou Suzette (Lenski), 69
The Beauties of the Children's Friend (Berquin), 100, 132
Beauty and the Beast, 143
Beinecke, Edwin J., 144
Beinecke Library, 140, 143, 145, 148
Beinecke, Walter, Jr., 146
Belanger, Terry, 112
Benet, Rosemary, 147
Berger, P., and T. Luckmann, *Social Construction of Reality*, 37
Bergman, Ingmar, 172
Berquin, Arnaud, *Beauties of the Children's Friend*, 100, 132
Bethel College, 81
Bewick, Thomas and John, 127
Bibliography, enumerative, 122
Bibliography of American Children's Books Printed Prior to 1821 (Welch), 95
Binding, 126–7, 132–3
Biograph Studios, 173, 178
Bizarre Sex, 160
Blondie and Dagwood, 159
Bluebeard, 142–3
Blum, John M., 50
Board games, 130
Board of Jewish Education Library, 85–6
Boob McNutt, 159
Bookselling, antiquarian, 99–100
Booktrade, eighteenth century, 125
Boreman, Thomas, 124
Boston Public Library, 189–91, 194
Boucicault, Nina, 147
The Boy Castaways (Barrie), 149
Boy Emigrants (Brooks), 56
Brackman, Jacob, 159
Brooks, Noah, *Boy Emigrants*, 56
Broomhilda, 163
Brown, Helen Gurley, 154
Browning, Robert, 143
Bugs Bunny, 159
Buhle, Paul, 160

Bund Archives of the Jewish Labor Movement, 84
Burk, Charlotte, 116
Burke, Kenneth, 38
Burnett, Frances Hodgson, 147
Burns, Lee, 106
Bushnell, Horace, 20
Burton, Richard (pseud.). See Nat Crouch, 124–5.
Burton, Robert (pseud.). See Nat Crouch, 124–5.

Cable, George W., 55; *Old Creole Days*, 56
Caley, Edmund, 147
The Cambridge Chronicle, 98
Campbell, John, 72
Canadiana, 80, 88
Caniff, Milton, 156
Captain America, 163–4
Cardell, William, 15, 28
Carleton and Porter, 26
Carroll, Lewis (pseud.). See Dodgson, Charles L.
Cawelti, John, *Decline of American Gentility*, 35
'Changes in the Style of Bookbinding 1550–1830' (Pollard), 126
Chapbooks, 130–1
Charlie Brown, 159
Chauvinism in children's literature, 5
Chicago Public Library, neglect of foreign language imprints, 81
Child, actors (motion picture), 173–4; and society, 5, 20; culture, 6, 8; labor laws, influences for, 177; nurture, author attitudes toward, 15–16
Childhood, attitudes toward, 20
Children, and motion pictures, 173; inner directed, 22
Children's books, anonymous, 130; bibliography, 132; dating of, 126–8; eighteenth century, 130–1; French, 132; preservation of, 100, 107; pseudonymous, 130
Children's Books in England and America in the 17th Century (Sloane), 123
Children's Books International, 191–2
Children's literature in research collections, 102, 105, 189, 190
Children's Services Division, American Library Association, 188
A Child's Garden of Verses (Stevenson), 146

Child's Moral Instructor, 124
Church, Benjamin, 129
Cinderella, 143
Cities. See Urbanization.
City Block (Frank), 63
Civil War, 18, 37, 49
Claude, 156
Cleaver, Vera and Bill, *Where the Lilies Bloom*, 61
Clemens, Samuel L., 'Jumping Frog of Calaveras County,' 57; *Huckleberry Finn*, 58
Cleveland Public Library, 81
Collecting practices of research libraries, 85–6, 89, 95–8, 101–02
Colonel Jack (Defoe), 123
Colvin, Sidney, 145
Combined Books USA, 191
Comenius, J. A., 131
Comics, American, 153–165
Committee on National Planning for Special Collections, 188
Community Motion Picture Bureau, 175
Competition for rare children's books, 102
The Conjurer, 124
Cooper, Mary, 124
Coover, Robert, 162
Cotton in My Sack (Lenski), 69
Couvay Brothers, 136 n. 23
Crane, Anthony, 144
Crane, Walter, 143–4, 148
The Cries of London, 124
Crouch, Nat, 124–5
Crumb, Robert, 160–2
'The Cry of the Children,' 176–7
Culture, maintenance of, 79
Cunha, George, 110–11, 115
Cutt, M. Nancy, *Mrs. Sherwood and Her Books for Children*, 129

Dame Wiggins of Lee, 139
Decline of American Gentility (Cawelti), 35
Decorated Book Papers (Loring), 127
Defoe, Daniel, 122, 154; *Colonel Jack*, 123; *Robinson Crusoe*, 130, 139
Dictionnaire des ouvrages anonymes (Barbier), 130
Diethylzinc vapor, 114
Dillard, Annie, 162
Disneyland, 161
Disney, Walt, 8; motion pictures, 71
The Distribution of Books by Catalogue from the Invention of Printing to A.D.

1800 (Pollard and Ehrman), 125
Doctorow, E. L., *Ragtime*, 70
Dodgson, Charles L., 142, 143, 148
Doonesbury, 163
Dornelles, Leny, 192
Dragonwings (Yep), 61
Dress, children's, 8
Dropouts, 163
'The Drunkard's Reformation,' 178
Dunbar, Janet, *J. M. Barrie, The Man Behind the Image*, 148
Dunton, John, 125

Edgeworth, Maria, 25, 29; correspondence, 139; *Frank*, 139; *Harry and Lucy*, 139
Edison, Thomas A., 172
Edward Morrill & Sons, *American Children's Books, 1723–1939 Catalogue Six*, 99, 100
Eesti Koolitoimkond (Estonian School Committee), 87
Eggleston, Edward, *The Hoosier School-Boy*, 56; *The Hoosier Schoolmaster*, 16
Eighteenth century books, bibliographical control of, 122
'Eight-Pagers,' 158
Elisabeth Ball Collection, 133–4
Emblem books, 130
Emerson, Ralph W., 65
Engelhardt, Steve, 164
English Woodcuts 1480–1535 (Hodnett), 128
Enright, Elizabeth, *The Saturdays*, 63–5
Eroticism in fiction, 153–4
Estonian children's literature, 82, 87–8
Ethnic minorities in literature, 73
Evans, Edmund, 143
The Evolution of Publisher's Binding Styles 1770–1900 (Sadlier), 126
Ewing, Mrs., 28

Fables, 26
The Fabulous Furry Freak Brothers, 160
Faith, 72
Falk, Lee, 156
Fantago, 160
The Fantastic Four, 159
Fantasy, 27, 71–2
A Father's Legacy (Gregory), 100
Fellini, Federico, 172
Fenton, Edward, 192
Fiction, adult, 60
Fiction, children's, anti-slavery sentiment

in, 18; Calvinism in, 19; characterization in, 16; class consciousness in, 27, 41, 50; development of, 29; dialect in, 56–8; gentility in, 37; in Jacksonian society, 19–22, 25; local color in, 55, 57–9; materialism in, 22; moral education in, 15–17, 19, 21, 23–4, 183; moral values in, 5, 21, 38; narrative in, 16, 17; nationalism in, 14, 184; optimism in, 14; origins in the United States, 14; plot in, 16; political issues in, 18; realistic, 5, 27; regionalism in, 55–75; regional setting in, 61, 63, 67–8; relation to adult fiction, 29; rural setting in, 59, 60, 63–5, 69; rural values in, 184; setting in, 16, 24, 56, 59; sex-role images in, 25; social consciousness in, 29; social issues in, 18, 19, 183–4; societal goals in, 14; urban setting in, 63–4, 70–1
Fiction, children's periodical, Civil War in, 51; discipline in, 48; ethnic minorities in, 48; gentry values in, 39–45; influence of, 50; militarism in, 51; moral values in, 38, 40–1; nationalism in, 49; relationship to adult fiction, 47
Fiction, teenage, 5
Fisher, Bud, 159
Fishman, Joshua, *Language Loyalty in the United States*, 79
Ford, Daniel Sharp, 40
Foreign language press, 79
The Forty Thieves, 143
Foster, Edith Dunham, 175
Foxon, David, *Thoughts on the History and Future of Bibliographical Description*, 129
Frank (Edgeworth), 139
Frankfurter Kolloquium, vii
Frank Leslie's Boys' and Girls' Weekly, 44
Frank, Waldo, *City Block*, 63
Fraser, James, 83, 189
Freaky Friday (Rodgers), 71
Free Library of Philadelphia, 96, 105
Fritz the Cat, 160
Fromm, Eric, 106

Gate, Ethel M., 147
Gay's Fables, 100
Gelfant, Blanche, 63
Gentility, gentry concept of, 42
Gentry, authors, American, 41–3; class, American, 38, 41–3; elite, American, 37, 42, 46; literature, British, 49;

values, American, 40–3
Germany, National Socialist period, 61
Giants in the Earth (Rolvaag), 60
Girl Fight Comics, 160
Goldsmith, Oliver, 130
Goodrich, Samuel, 16
Gordon, Flash, 156–7
Grahame, Kenneth, Wind in the Willows,
    147
Gratz, Simon, 97
Gray, Euphemia, 140
Gray, Harold, 159
Greenaway, Emerson, 96–7
Greenaway, Kate, 147
Green, Justin, 162
Gregory, John, A Father's Legacy, 100
Grey, Jill, Sarah Fielding: The Governess
    or Little Female Academy, 129
Griffin, Gillett, 134
Griffith, D. W., 173–4, 178
Gustavus Adolphus College, 81

Hagar the Horrible, 163
Hairbreadth Harry, 155
Halkett, S., and J. Laing, Dictionary of
    Anonymous and Pseudonymous English
    Literature, 130
Happy Hooligan, 158
Harriet the Spy (Fitzhugh), 71
Harris, Joel C., Uncle Remus, 56–7
Harry and Lucy (Edgeworth), 139
'Harry and Lucy' (Ruskin), 140
Harte, Bret, 55; 'Luck of Roaring Camp,'
    56
Haugen, Einar, Norwegian Language in
    America, 79
Haviland, Virginia, 121
Hayes, Ruth, 189
'Head comics,' 159
Heartman, Charles F., New England
    Primer Issued Prior to 1830, 99
Hebrew children's literature, 85–6
Henley, William Earnest, 145–6
Henne, Frances, viii
Herriman, George, 159
Hill, Octavia, 143
Hodnett, Edward, English Woodcuts
    1480–1535, 128
The Holy Bible Abridged, 101
Hoosier School-Boy (Eggleston), 56
Hoosier Schoolmaster (Eggleston), 16
The House of Seven Gables (Hawthorne),
    66
Howells, William D., 47
Howerla Publishing Co., 89–90

Hughes, Thomas, 147; Tom Brown's
    School Days, 50
Hunter, Mollie, 192
Hymns for the Amusement of Children
    (Smart), 127

The Immediate Experience (Warshow),
    159
Immigrants in North America, 79
Imperatives, cultural, 37
Industrialization, author attitudes toward,
    18
Ingelow, Jean, 49–50
An Inland Voyage (Stevenson), 144
Inner City Romance, 160
International Board on Books for Young
    People, vii
'The International Comix Conspiracy'
    (Brackman), 159
International Institute for Children's and
    Youth Literature and Reading Research,
    vii
Internationalism in children's literature, 5
International Research Society for Chil-
    dren's and Youth Literature, vii
Irving, Washington, 13
Isaac Watts: Divine Songs Attempted in
    Easy Language for the Use of Children
    (Pafford), 129

Jack and Jill, 48
Jack and Jill (Alcott), 41
Jacksonian society, 13, 14, 21–2
Jackson, William A., 'Printed Wrappers
    of the Fifteenth to the Eighteenth Cen-
    turies,' 126
James, Henry, 66
Jewett, Sarah O., 57, 65
Jewish Book Annual, 84
Jewish Education Committee, 83
Jewish Theological Seminary Library of
    New York; 85
Jiggs, 159
J. M. Barrie. The Man Behind the Image
    (Dunbar), 148
Johnson and Warner, 95
Johnson, Jacob, 95
Johnson, Richard, 129
'Jo-Jo Books,' 158
Jones, Howard Mumford, 192
Jordon, Alice M., 190
Juan and Juanita (Baylor), 58
Judy's Journey (Lenski), 69

Kahles, Charles, 155–6

Kazdan, Hayyim, 83
Kelly, George, 114
Kern, Alexander, 35
Kilner, Dorothy, 129
Kilner, Mary Ann, 129
Kinderzeitung, 87
Kinetoscope, 173
The King of the Golden River (Ruskin), 140
Kingsley, Charles, 143
'The Kleptomaniac,' 178
Knock on Any Door (Motley), 63
Kraus-Thomson, Ltd., 107
Krazy Kat, 159

Lang, Andrew, 147
Language maintenance, 79, 83; Armenian, 90–1
Langwell Vapor-Phase, 114
Larcom, Lucy, 48
Latvian children's literature, 87–8
Lear, Edward, 140
Lee and Shepard, 26
Lee, Harper, *To Kill a Mockingbird*, 61
Legends for Lionel (Crane), 143
Lenski, Lois, *Bayou Suzette*, 69; *Cotton in My Sack*, 69; *Judy's Journey*, 69
Letters from a Father to His Son (Aikin), 100
Lewis, C.S., 72
Library of Congress, 86, 88, 102, 113, 114–15
The Life and Errors of John Dunton (Dunton), 125
Li'l Abner, 163
Linton, William James, 141, 143
Lithuanian children's literature, 87
'Little House Books.' See Wilder, Laura I.
'Little House on the Prairie' (TV series), 70
Little Lord Fauntleroy (Burnett), 49
Little Orphan Annie, 159
The Little Red Hen, 26
Little Red Riding Hood, 106
Little Red Riding Hood: A Terror Tale of the Nursery (Weiss), 105
The Little White Bird (Barrie), 146
Little Women (Alcott), 16
Livermore, George, 98
Locke, John, 131
Longman, Green and Co., 146
Lord, Albert, 193
Loring, Rosamond, *Decorated Book Papers*, 127
'Luck of Roaring Camp' (Harte), 56

Lumière, Auguste, 172
Luther College, 81

M'Carty and Davis, 95
MacDonald, George, 141–3
MacDonald, Greville, 148
MacKenzie, D. F., 'Printers of the Mind,' 129
McKerrow, R.B., *Printers' and Publishers' Devices in England and Scotland 1485–1640*, 128
Mainau Conferences, vii
Malgi, Meemi, 87
Mandrake, 156
Manuscripts, preservation of, 148
Marshall, John, 124
Mass market children's literature, 7
Mass media and the socialization process, 38
Maverick, Peter, 101
Mayhew, Edgar, viii, ix
Mekhitarist Library, 91
Méliès, Georges, 172
Merriwell, Frank, 51
Mickey Mouse, 159
Microfilming of early children's books, 107
Midland Rare Book Company, 96
Milne, A.A., 147
Minnesota State Historical Society, 81
Mission imprints, 98
Mrs. Pleasant's Story Book, 101
Mrs. Sherwood and Her Books for Children (Cutt), 129
Mr. Michael Mouse Unfolds His Tale (Crane), 144
Mr. Natural, 160
Mizumura, Kazue, 192
Modern Language Association, viii
A Moral Tale (MacLeod), 45
Morpholine vapor, 113
Mother Was a Lady (Kelly), 35, 47
Motion pictures, 174–6, 178
Motley, Willard, *Knock on Any Door*, 63
Moulton, Priscilla, 189
Muir, P.H., 124, 132
Mumford, Lewis, 60
Mutt and Jeff, 159
'My Favorite Erotic Experience,' 154
Myths, 65, 70

National libraries and children's literature, 80, 88
National Library of Canada, 80, 88, 114

National Planning Committee for Special Collections, Children's Services Division, American Library Association, viii
New and Complete System of Arithmetic (Pike), 100
Newbery, John, 124
New Cambridge Bibliography of English Literature, 121
New England Document Conservation Center, 111, 115
New England Primer, 98
New England Primer Issued Prior to 1830 (Heartman), 99
New York Public Library, Central Children's Room, foreign language books in, 81, 89; Jewish Division, juvenile Yiddica and Hebraica in, 85–6; Research Division, children's literature in, 81, 89; Thompkins Square Branch, foreign language books in, 89
Nixon, Howard M., *Styles and Designs of Bookbinding from the Twelfth to the Twentieth Century*, 127
Nonsense Songs, Stories, Botany, and Alphabets (Lear), 140
'Nostalgia craze,' 70
Nylander, Jane, viii, ix

Ochrana, 84
October Revolution, 84
Old and Rare Children's Books (Schatzki), 99
Old Creole Days (Cable), 56
Oldham, C. B., 128
Oliver Optic's Magazine, 46
Opie, Iona and Peter, 121, 130
Oppenheimer, Edgar S., 102, n. 2
Opper, Frederick Burr, 'Happy Hooligan,' 158
Organ, Robert, 115
The Origin, History and Character of the New England Primer (Livermore), 98
Osborne Collection, 105, 124
Osbourne, Lloyd, 144–5
Our Young Folks, 36, 43, 45, 47–8, 50
Oxford Bibliographical Society, 124

Pafford, N. H. P., *Isaac Watts: Divine Songs Attempted in Easy Language for the Use of Children*, 129
Palooka, Joe, 156, 158
Pamela (Richardson), 153–5
Pamela's Daughters (Utter and Needham), 154

Paris, John A., *Philosophy in Sport Made Science in Earnest*, 173
Park, Robert E., *The Immigrant Press and Its Control*, 79
Patterson, Catharine Tinker, 144
Peacock at Home (Dorset), 139
Peanuts (Schulz), 159
Pellowski, Anne, 189
Penny Whistles (Stevenson), 145
Periodicals, children's, British contributors in, 49; circulation of, 45; Hebrew language, 86; title changes in, 46; Ukrainian, 89; Yiddish, 86
Perrault, Charles, 106; 'Little Red Riding Hood,' 105
Persons, Stow, 35, 37
Peter and Wendy (Barrie), 146
Peter Pan (Barrie), 146–7, 149
'Peter Pan' crackers, 147
Peter Pan in Kensington Gardens (Barrie), 146–7
'Peter Pan' playing cards, 147
The Phantom, 156
Phillipps, Sir Thomas, 101
Philosophy in Sport Made Science in Earnest (Paris), 173
Physical and Chemical Properties of Book Papers (Barrow Laboratory), 112
Picture book development, 131
Pierpont Morgan Library, 121, 127, 133
Pike, Nicholas, *New and Complete System of Arithmetic*, 100
Pilgrim's Progress (Bunyan), 142
Plumb, J. H., 131
Poesio, Carla, 192
Pogo, 159, 163
Pollard, G., *Changes in the Style of Bookbinding, 1550–1830*, 126
Pollard, G., and A. Ehrman, *Distribution of Books by Catalogue, from the Invention of Printing to A.D. 1800*, 125
Pollard and Redgrave, *Short-Title Catalog*, 122–3
Polock, Moses, 95, 98
Poole, Frazer, 113
Pope-Hennessy, James, 148
Popeye, 156, 159
Popular Culture Association, viii
Pothooks and Perseverance (Crane), 143
Potter, Beatrix, 8
Praeterita (Ruskin), 139
Preservation, of book and paper, 105–114; centers and laboratories for, 117; of motion pictures, 170; training programs for, 112, 115–6

Price, Franklin, 96
Prince Valiant, 156
The Princess and Curdie (MacDonald), 141
The Princess and the Goblin (MacDonald), 141
'Printed Wrappers of the Fifteenth to the Eighteenth Century' (Jackson), 126
Printers' and Publishers' Devices in England and Scotland 1485–1640 (McKerrow), 128
Publishers of children's books, American Sunday School Union, 26, 96; Boreman, Thomas, 124; Carleton and Porter, 26; Cooper, Mary, 124; Crouch, Nat, 124–5; Jacob Johnson, 95; Johnson and Warner, 95; Lee and Shepard, 26; Longmans, Green and Co., 146; M'Carty and Davis, 95; Marshall, John, 124; Newbery, John, 124; Sunday and Adult School Union, 96
Publishing, in minority languages in the United States, 81–2; of children's books, eighteenth century, 124–5
Punctuation Personified, 96–7

Rackham, Arthur, 146–7
Radio broadcasting, children's, 7
Ragtime (Doctorow), 70
Rawlings, Marjorie K., *The Yearling*, 61–2, 65
Raymond, Alex, 156–7
R. B. (pseud.). See Nat Crouch, 124–5.
Readex Microprint Corporation, 107
Ready, William, 193
Rebecca of Sunnybrook Farm (Wiggin), 57
Regeneration Through Violence (Slotkin), 154
Regnal, 113
Research, in children's literature, 3, 4, 5, 7, 8; resources for, 185
Richardson, Samuel, *Pamela*, 153, 155; *Sir Charles Grandison*, 130
The Rise of the Novel (Watt), 154
The Riverside Magazine for Young People, 36, 40, 43
Robinson Crusoe (Defoe), 130, 139
Robinson, Jerry, *The Comics*, 158
Rodgers, Mary, *Freaky Friday*, 71
Rogers, Buck, 156
Roll, Dušan, 193
Rolvaag, O. E., *Giants in the Earth*, 60
Roosevelt, Theodore, 50
Roscoe, Sydney, 124

Rosenbach, A. S. W., 95–8, 101
Rosenbach Collection of Early American Children's Books (Free Library of Philadelphia), 95, 97, 99, 102
Rousseau, Jean Jacques, 132
Rowlf, 160
The Rule of the New Creature, 97
Ruskin, John, childhood reading, 139; 'Harry and Lucy,' 140; *The King of the Golden River*, 140; manuscripts, 140; *Praeterita*, 139
Ryland, Edward, 124

Sabin, Joseph, 100
Sadlier, Michael, *The Evolution of Publishers' Binding Styles 1770–1900*, 126
St. John, Judith, 105; *The Osborne Collection of Early Children's Books*, 124
St. Nicholas, 37, 39, 43, 45–6, 48
Sarah Fielding: The Governess or Little Female Academy (Grey), 129
The Saturdays (Enright), 63
Schaefer, Jack, *Shane*, 61
Schatzki, Walter, *Old and Rare Children's Books*, 99
Schulz, Charles M., 8; *Peanuts*, 159
Science fiction, 71–2
Scientific Dialogues (Joyce), 139
Scout groups as publishers, 87–8
Scudder, Horace, 40
Self-Willed Susie, 16
Service Bureau for Jewish Education, 83, 86
Sex in popular literature, 162
Shaffer, Ellen, 96
Shane (Schaefer), 61
Shelley, Percy B., 146
Shelton, Gilbert, 160
Sholem Aleichem Folk Institute, 83, 86
Short Ribs, 163
Simmons College, viii; School of Library Science, 188–9
Sineath, Timothy, viii
Sir Charles Grandison (Richardson), 130
Slateandpencilvania (Crane), 143
Sloane, William, *Children's Books in England and America in the Seventeenth Century*, 123
Slotkin, Richard, *Regeneration Through Violence*, 154
Smart, Christopher, *Hymns for the Amusement of Children*, 127
Smith, Richard, 114
Smithsonian Institution, Office of Museum Programs, 115

Social change, 66–7; in Jacksonian society, 21

The Social Construction of Reality (Berger and Luckmann), 37

Social Darwinism, 30

Socialization, primary, 38

Society and children's literature, 36, 186–7

Soltes, Mordecai, *The Yiddish Press*, 79

Sotheby & Co., 99

Spencer, Isobel, 148

Spradley, James, 36

State historical societies, 80–1

State libraries, 80

der Stephanian, Silva, 91

Stevenson, Robert L., 144–6, 148; *An Inland Voyage*, 144; *Penny Whistles*, 145; *Travels With a Donkey*, 144

Stone, Wilbur Macy, 134

Story of a Bad Boy (Aldrich), 16, 47, 56

Stover, Dink, 51

Street literature, 130

Stueart, Robert, viii

Styles and Designs of Bookbinding from the Twelfth to the Twentieth Century (Nixon), 127

Subject Collections (Ash), 80

Summer in a Cañon (Wiggin), 56

Sunday and Adult School Union, 96

Suomi College, 81

Superman, 156

Svoboda, 89, 90

Swann Galleries, 98–101, 102 n. 2

Symposia, children's literature research, vii

Tannhauser Company, 177

Tarzan, 156

Television, children's, 7

Thoreau, Henry D., 51

Thoughts on the History and Future of Bibliographical Description (Foxon), 129

Thumb, Thomas, 130

Thurber, Mrs. Dexter, 174–5

Tighe, Benjamin, 102 n. 2

'Tijuana Bibles,' 158

Tinker, Chauncey Brewster, 144

Toffler, Alvin, 67

To Kill a Mockingbird (Lee), 61

Toledo Public Library, 81

Tolkien, J. R. R., 72

Tom Brown's School Days (Hughes), 50

Tommy Thoroughgood, 101

Tom Sawyer (Clemens), 16

Townsend, John Rowe, 69–70

Tracy, Dick, 156

Trancendentalism, 69

Travels with a Donkey (Stevenson), 144

Trevelyan, Hilda, 146

Tuan, Yi-Fu, 65

Turner, Frederick Jackson, 71

Ukrainian Academy of Arts and Sciences, 89

Ukrainian children's literature, 82, 88–90

Ukrainian National Association, 90

Ukrainian National Library and Museum (Chicago), 89

Ukrainian National Women's Association, 90

Uncle Remus (Harris), 56–57, 68

United States Food and Drug Administration, 114

Urbanization, attitudes toward, 18

Vaba Eesti Soña, 88

Values, developmental, 5; transmission of, 43

Veselka, 89

'Victorianism,' 49

Vigilante motif, 5

Viguers, Ruth Hill, 190

Walker, Bernard, 113

Walpole, Horace, 140

'The Waltons' (TV series), 70

Warshow, Robert, *The Immediate Experience*, 159

Washington, George, 18

Waters, Peter, 115

Watt, Ian, *Rise of the Novel*, 154

Weedon, M. J. P., 129

Weisburger, Elizabeth, 114

Weiss, Harry, *Little Red Riding Hood: A Terror Tale of the Nursery*, 105

Wei T'o Spray, 114

Welch, d'Alté, *Bibliography of American Children's Books Printed Prior to 1821*, 95, 99, 100

Welty, Eudora, 66–7

Wessen, Ernest, Jr., 96

Where the Lilies Bloom (Cleaver), 61, 68

Wide Awake, 36, 43

Wiggin, Kate D., 65; *Rebecca of Sunnybrook Farm*, 57; *A Summer in a Cañon*, 56

Wilder, Laura, 'Little House Books,' 61–63, 65

Wily Coyote, 159

Wilson, S. Clay, 161–2
Wing, *Short-Title Catalog*, 122–3
Wishy, Bernard, 35–6
Wittke, Carl, *The German Language Press in America*, 79
W. J. Barrow Laboratory, 112, 113, 115, 116
Wonderful Wizard of Oz (Baum), 58–9
Wonder Wart Hog, 160
Workmen's Circle, 83, 86–7
Workmen's Circle Education Department, 86
The World Turned Up-Side Down, 124
The Writer, 48

Yale University Library, 139
The Yearling (Rawlings), 61, 63
Year's Work in Early Children's Book Studies, 131
Yep, Laurence, *Dragonwings*, 61
Yiddish children's literature, 85–7, 90
Yiddish language schools, 83
Yivo Institute for Jewish Research, 84–85
The Young Child's ABC, 100
Youth's Companion, 36, 40, 43, 45–6, 48

Zap, 160

SOCIETY & CHILDREN'S LITERATURE

has been composed by Cambridge Linoterm in Sabon, a face designed by Jan Tschichold. The roman is based on a fount engraved by Garamond and the italic on a fount by Granjon, but Tschichold introduced many refinements to make these models suitable for contemporary typographic needs. Designed by Ann Schroeder, the book was printed on an acid-free sheet, Warren's Olde Style, by the Murray Printing Company. Jacket and title page calligraphy is by Tim Girvin.